# The Global Carbon Crisis

Emerging Carbon Constraints and Strategic Management Options

# THE GLOBAL CARBON CRISIS

## Emerging Carbon Constraints and Strategic Management Options

**Timo Busch** and **Paul Shrivastava**

Routledge
Taylor & Francis Group

LONDON AND NEW YORK

First published 2011 by Greenleaf Publishing Limited

Published 2017 by Routledge
2 Park Square, Milton Park, Abingdon, Oxon OX14 4RN
711 Third Avenue, New York, NY 10017, USA

*Routledge is an imprint of the Taylor & Francis Group, an informa business*

British Library Cataloguing in Publication Data:
    Busch, Timo.
        Emerging carbon constraints and strategic management
        options. -- (The global carbon crisis ; v. 1)
        1. Carbon dioxide mitigation. 2. Industries--Environmental
        aspects. 3. Industries--Social aspects.
        I. Title II. Series
        658.4'083-dc22

    ISBN-13: 978-1-906093-61-7 (hbk)

# Contents

# Acknowledgments

This book would not have been possible without the support and help of many people and organizations. We want to acknowledge the support of several institutions and individuals involved in the development process. We thank the students and faculty at ETH, Zurich, and Concordia University, Montreal, the institutions where this project lived for nearly two years.

We acknowledge the David O'Brien Centre for Sustainable Enterprise at Concordia University for the support of Timo Busch's visit to Montreal, where the main part of this manuscript was finalized.

Several individuals helped us in developing, reviewing, and strengthening this book. We would like to thank Stephanie Berger, Grace Goss-Durant, Volker Hoffmann, Andrew Ross and Malte Schneider, for feedback and editing support on earlier versions of the manuscript. The team from Greenleaf Publishing, notably John Stuart, Dean Bargh, and Gillian Bourn, provided professional advice and support at every stage of this book's development.

Finally, a big thank you to our spouses, Nina Busch and Michelle Cooper, for putting up with us while we were away from home and family working on the manuscript.

# Introduction

The motivation behind this book is simple. For at least a decade the science of climate change has warned us of the dire need for action. And action is needed from the corporate sector, which is the main engine of economic production and consumption. Yet managerial and corporate understanding of climate change and related energy issues remains fragmented, incomplete, and lacks the urgency this problem deserves. So, this is a book for a corporate and academic audience: managers in business as well as teachers of our business students—the managers of tomorrow's businesses. It brings climate change and energy discussions to the corporate context in a business framework and language.

In the past, the environment of business was seen as constituted largely of economic, technological, regulatory and political, and social and cultural forces. To a much lesser extent it included the "natural" environment as a source of raw materials, and as a compliance issue. Costs associated with environmental issues were erroneously understood to be small and were generally externalized out of company accounts.

Discussions regarding climate change and finite fossil fuel reserves of the past two decades have reversed the order of importance of these elements. Climate change has caused the environment of business to change completely and permanently. Similarly, we are on the verge of depleting natural fossil fuel reserves. Now the natural environment issues of resource availability, fossil energy, carbon sinks, and climate are driving economic choices. Now we understand that the—not yet fully internalized—carbon costs are very high and there is both public expectation and government regulation for corporations to deal with them internally. There is a whole new economy—the low-carbon economy—on the horizon. Yet our production and consumption patterns still remain in a carbon-locked position. This results in the risk that a global carbon crisis will emerge.

There are many parallels between the global financial crisis and a potential carbon crisis. The main message of this book in this regard is: similar to the financial crisis, the carbon crisis would have broad and severe implications for humanity. And we were aware of this before both crises sparked off. The difference between the two crises is that we cannot reverse the effects of climate change and fossil fuel scarcity as easily as we can repair the global financial system. Therefore, tackling the issues early enough is even more important in the carbon crisis context.

To address important changes in the business environment, firms need to be aware of the consequences that a changing climate and finite carbon resources will have on their business performance. The element carbon—as a resource and as emissions—is both a threat and an opportunity for companies. It is an economic threat for carbon-intensive production systems. They will need to be changed to avoid further harmful climatic change and because of the limited availability of carbon-based fuels on our planet. New opportunities emerge for companies that can creatively design and produce goods and services that fit the emerging carbon-constrained business environment. Many sectors of the economy, for example renewable energy, energy and resources conservation, waste reduction and management, and carbon finance markets, will expand rapidly, as others that are carbon- and resource-intensive enter into decline. Corporate managers are well served by understanding the sources of opportunities and threats and business models that will help them transition their own companies to prosper in carbon-constrained environments.

This book has several modest goals. It does not explain climate "science" and global energy issues in detail. These are huge areas of study with thousands of researchers and hundreds of journals.

Highly competent and comprehensive insights about climate science and energy developments are available in the form of reports: for example, by the IPCC (Intergovernmental Panel on Climate Change) and the IEA (International Energy Agency). Instead, our purpose is to translate important insights from the natural sciences, economics, and equity discussions, for the corporate audience. As such, we briefly review important aspects of these discussions and elaborate on sources of misunderstanding with respect to climate change and fossil fuel availability and their business implications.

Discussions of climate change outside the scientific domain are often confusing, uncertain, and politically complex. They do not encourage action. This was most evident in the December 2009 Climate Treaty discussions in Copenhagen. Ultimately, we did not get an international treaty, which taught us an important lesson. Since we were impelled to write this book by the urgency to act on climate change, after Copenhagen we see more than ever the need for simple, direct, and effective solutions. While writing the book, the summit in Cancun, Mexico, one year later, further illustrated that international climate policy presents a serious diplomatic challenge—unfortunately at the expense of concrete action. So our goal here is to remain pragmatic and offer solutions that policy makers and corporate managers can implement. With this book we want to provoke action, thoughtful action, intended to develop and establish a low-carbon future for companies and society.

The strategic management options we discuss include choices for corporate management, and wider societal choices. The strategic perspective we adopt is long-term and holistic. We believe solutions intended to prevent a global carbon crisis need to be systemic and address all aspects of society, not just the economy or certain technologies. And we need solutions that will endure over the long term. There are no quick fixes for such globally interconnected issues. Using a strategic, farsighted perspective, we discuss actions targeted at establishing a low-carbon society through leverages at three levels. At the macro level, we discuss the importance of stringent industrial policies for climate change and propose the idea of an international carbon-equal fund. At the meso level, we elaborate on the role of inter-firm collaborations for establishing low-carbon industries and production systems. At the micro level, we illustrate the virtue of proactive carbon strategies and suggest a corporate carbon management framework. We believe there is plenty for all of us to do at personal, organizational, community, national, and international levels. We are also convinced that it is possible—albeit challenging—to implement an orderly transition to a sustainable global economy. Companies will be one of the main vehicles for these transformations. The book offers one approach for repositioning our business models to thrive beyond carbon constraints and help prevent a global carbon crisis.

# Part I
# A strategic view of carbon constraints

# 1

# The two sides of the carbon coin

Carbon is a basic element of life on Earth. It is the most abundant element, one on which many life systems depend, and a primary source of energy (fossil fuels). Today carbon is in huge turmoil—humans are on their way to creating a global carbon crisis. Eons of stable transformation and retransformation of carbon on Earth are now being destabilized by anthropogenic activities. Large human populations, their habitats, production and consumption processes are leading to a significant overuse of the element carbon. Excessive use of non-renewable, carbon-based fuels has caused excessive emissions of carbon dioxide into the Earth's atmosphere.

The phenomenon of high crude oil and gas prices coupled with the prevailing public and scientific debate about climate change have one thing in common: both center on carbon. Despite carbon abundance in the atmosphere as carbon dioxide, there are limited resources of it in its useable form for fossil fuels. In other words, carbon is accumulating in the wrong forms and in the wrong place. Historically, carbon naturally accumulated in the ground in great quantities over geologic timescales; now, however, this quantity is being transferred to the atmosphere in a comparatively short time period. This ongoing process has accelerated, and as such contributes to the emergence of a new industrial crisis (Shrivastava *et al.* 1988): the global carbon crisis.

Overcoming the dependency on fossil fuels and significantly reducing greenhouse gas emissions has been recognized as one of the major challenges of the 21st century. However, global energy consumption continues to expand. A United Nations (UN 2007) report estimates that there has been an increase of 20 percent since 1990. Although progress has been achieved in developing and using cleaner energy technologies, the majority of current energy sources remain carbon-based. The amount of fossil-fuel-based energy consumption dropped in OECD countries from 94 percent in 1960 to 81 percent in 2009, while at the same time the total energy use almost tripled.[1] Today, energy from established renewable energy sources, such as hydropower and biofuels, accounts for only about 12 percent of total energy consumption, whereas newer technologies relying on wind, solar, wave, and geothermal energy account for only 0.5 percent of total energy consumption (UN 2007). Nevertheless, it is particularly important to recognize the possible strategies at hand in order to prevent a full-blown carbon crisis, as was the case with the global financial crisis; thus it is important to start managing carbon strategically and with foresight. This holds for policy makers and firms, as well as individual consumers—everyone has his or her stake in the emerging global carbon crisis.

This book stresses the role of firms and industrial production processes in the context of the carbon crisis. Both entities represent a fundamental portion of the carbon dilemma while simultaneously are most affected by its emerging constraints. We argue that managers need to be aware of the relevance of an emerging carbon crisis for their business environment and that proactive responses to this crisis are urgently required, from a business standpoint (Lovins *et al.* 2005; Stern 2006) as well as in terms of social responsibility (UNDP 2007). Notably, we stress that climate change and dependency on fossil fuels are related business topics that need to be managed

---

1 World Development Indicators: data.worldbank.org/indicator (accessed February 17, 2011). In 1960 the OECD countries' energy use was about 1,924 million tons of oil equivalent; in 2009 this was about 5,230 million tons, which corresponds to an increase of 172 percent.

simultaneously. When intensifying efforts to prevent a potential climate collapse, the adverse effects stemming from mismanaging fossil fuels can be preempted at the same time. Companies and their value chains are implicated in climate processes through their products, production systems, logistical systems, and consumption of energy and natural resources. As a result, every industry and company is exposed to climate change risks, though to different degrees and intensities. At the same time, companies also face strategic business opportunities arising from the necessary reconstruction of our economies towards a low-carbon system. By proactively addressing climate change challenges, companies can mitigate risks and gain competitive advantages. To do so, there are three core elements, which this book successively explores: (1) understanding carbon-induced changes in the business environment; (2) identifying the key issues and challenges ahead; and (3) illustrating strategic options in order to manage the issues adequately and effectively.

The first part of the book looks at carbon- and climate-related changes in the business environment. For corporate management, recognizing this change is pertinent especially in cases involving managerial decisions with long-term implications. It is an important first step towards acknowledging that the business environment is shifting towards a low-carbon society. Although this shift has created new risks for corporate management, it has also generated new low-carbon business opportunities, especially in the long run. To seriously consider carbon-induced risks and opportunities in one's business there must be substantive redefinition of strategic management thinking: seemingly well-established business structures need to be revised and new business models need to be explored systematically.

The second part of the book identifies sources of emerging carbon constraints and elaborates on the likely consequences of a global carbon crisis. Current reporting in the media about climate change points towards the dominance of two contrasting positions: skeptical analyses that question the general validity of climate change as a scientifically proven effect; and exaggerations that climate change will have devastating and dramatic consequences for humanity and the entire planet. Both of these positions are misleading because they undermine the scientific integrity of a very sound and valid natural phenomenon, climate change, which we will elaborate on in more detail in the second part. However, as a consequence of prevailing differences on this topic, managers are often faced with difficulty in deciding what sources of information are trustworthy and credible. Generally, it is important to distinguish between two basic positions in this context: a position that legitimately understands the basic scientific foundation and proposes concrete and implementable mitigation and/or adaptation measures for addressing climate change; and a position that embellishes or tries to vilify climate change science in the media. Managers need to be aware of these positions and cautious about unreliable sources.

Therefore, providing insights into the basic scientific foundation and opting for enhanced transparency on the carbon challenge ahead is especially important. In the ecology literature, there have been several efforts to make the public aware of the basic scientific processes that govern our natural environment and the ecological challenges that lie ahead. Scholars concerned about the natural environment such as Kenneth Boulding, Donella and Dennis Meadows, and Herman Daly published their analyses in the early '70s. They highlighted the fact that humanity faced natural limits to growth. Table 1 summarizes their main contributions. Although their concepts and models were correct on a theoretical basis, critics have pointed out that their warnings were premature and exaggerated given that future technologies temporarily solved some of the problems of growth. In fact, the doomsday scenarios that were put forward did not materialize. Nevertheless, these early studies inspired many more investigations in the realm of human-ecology systems and developments of corresponding concepts. One of the most recent studies was initiated by the G8 and five major developing countries. The main premise of the study entitled "The Economics of Ecosystems and Biodiversity" is that all businesses depend on biodiversity and ecosystem services (TEEB 2010). As such, the natural environment impacts businesses in both positive and negative ways and it is important to measure and quantify these impacts. In the second part of this book, we illustrate how the carbon and climate change issues, covered by past literature on potential ecological collapse, have been more accurate than

Table 1 **Overview of important contributions in the literature on ecological limits and crises**

Source: Boulding 1966; Meadows *et al*. 1972; Daly 1973

| | |
|---|---|
| Kenneth Boulding (1966) *The Economics of the Coming Spaceship Earth* | • The Earth of the future requires a shift in principles considering the world no longer as an open but as a closed economy<br><br>• The open economy can be considered as a "cowboy" economy, the cowboy being associated with the unlimited plains and also with reckless, exploitative, romantic, and violent behavior<br><br>• The closed economy can be considered as a "spaceman" economy, in which the Earth has become a single spaceship, without unlimited reservoirs for extraction or for pollution, and in which cyclical ecological systems are important |
| Dennis Meadows *et al*. (1972) *The Limits to Growth* | • Very little attention had been paid to the environmental consequences of economic growth. That will have to change in the future owing to limitations to growth<br><br>• The world economy is represented as a single economy. Five major interconnected trends between that economy and its environment are investigated: accelerating industrialization, rapid population growth, widespread malnutrition, depletion of non-renewable resources, and deteriorating natural environment<br><br>• With a system dynamics model the authors showed that growth patterns of the past cannot be extended into the future |
| Herman Daly (1973) *Toward a Steady-State Economy* | • A steady-state economy is defined by constant stock of physical wealth (artifacts) and a constant population, each maintained at some chosen, desirable level by a low rate of throughput<br><br>• The throughput is the inevitable cost of maintaining the stocks of people and artifacts and should be minimized subject to the maintenance of a chosen level of stocks. The throughput is controlled at its input (depletion) rather than at the pollution end<br><br>• Progress in the steady state consists in increasing ultimate efficiency (= service/throughput) by maintaining the stock with less throughput or getting more service per unit of time from the same stock |

previously anticipated and economists have now started to calculate the corresponding costs to society. We elaborate on how a global carbon crisis is now unfolding which will negatively affect businesses, prompting urgent action to mitigate these impacts.

In the third part of the book we illustrate strategic options that, if adequately managed, may help to prevent a global carbon crisis. We suggest two key mechanisms for an accelerated path towards a low-carbon society: adequate political enforcements on the macro (societal) level; and voluntary carbon reduction initiatives on the meso (inter-organizational) level and micro (firm) level. These management options target two key technological challenges: the relationship between economic growth and energy demand; and the level of carbonization in the energy mix. To explain the logic behind this we refer to the famous equation by Ehrlich and Holdren (1971):

$$\text{Impact} = \text{Population} \times \text{Consumption} \times \text{Technology}$$

Following this formula, any potential impact of human beings on the ecological system can be explained by a function of the number of people living on the Earth, the per capita consumption, and the technology used to produce goods and services. The implications of this equation are illustrated in the greenhouse gases reduction target formulated by the European Union and the G8 in July 2009. The objective is that developed nations should pursue cuts of greenhouse gases of at least 80 percent below 1990 levels by 2050 (ECF 2010). In other words the impact in 2050—measured in terms of the carbon loading in the environment—shall only be about one-fifth of the 1990 level. Next, let us follow the majority of the population forecasts and assume that in 2050 the world population will be about nine billion, compared with six billion at the start of the century. This is a 50 percent increase in population. The average consumption per capita can be displayed by the gross domestic product (GDP) per capita. Let's assume there is an annual gross domestic product increase rate of 1.5 percent. This roughly corresponds to a doubling of gross domestic product by 2050. Applying the Ehrlich and Holdren formula delivers the following results: maintaining the current ecological impact (i.e. the current level of greenhouse gases) will require technological improvements of a factor of three.

Meeting the European Union's goal of reductions of 80 percent from the 1990 level of greenhouse gases (GHG) will require technological improvements by a factor of 15. To illustrate these technological challenges further, we can extend the original equation in the carbon context (also referred to as the "Kaya identity," coined by the Japanese energy economist Yoichi Kaya):

$$\text{GHG} = \text{Population} \times \text{GDP/Population} \times \text{Energy/GDP} \times \text{GHG/Energy}$$

It is important to emphasize that this equation is not a math function in terms of an increase in "x" has an effect on "y". All terms can be canceled out and then the simple message would be GHG = GHG. Thus, the purpose of the equation is illustration. It shows what determines the amount of GHG emissions. For example, if we want to curb GHG emissions by a certain percent, then the formula shows that we either have to stop population growth, reduce the amount of GDP per capita, reduce energy intensity of GDP, or improve the carbon intensity of the energy mix. Based on the latter two aspects, it can be demonstrated that the world economies face two central technological challenges in terms of global carbon management. First, there is the need to decouple economic growth and energy demand. In a world with steadily increasing production and consumption it is important that economic growth does not necessarily parallel energy use. This "decoupling factor" is displayed in the quotient "Energy/GDP." Second, the energy produced needs to be based on low-carbon or renewable energy sources. Only a significant decarbonization of the energy mix will yield the technological progress by a factor X that is required in order to avoid further threats to the global climate system. This "decarbonization factor" can be displayed in the quotient "GHG/Energy." In conclusion, we have to be aware of the challenge ahead and its potential solutions. The emergence of a global carbon crisis would significantly affect the business environment; both the decoupling and the decarbonization factors should be considered as important conditions for a country's long-term competitiveness.

# 2
# Emerging carbon constraints

In this chapter we discuss how companies are implicated in the global carbon crisis. We use the term "carbon constraints" in a broad sense to refer to limitations regarding established utilization patterns of the element carbon and the corresponding impacts on business conditions. These limitations pertain to direct, physical effects as well as to indirect, human-induced effects. Furthermore, they also involve carbon-related feedback loops, which comprise impacts on weather, river and mountain systems, and agriculture. As such, our use of "carbon" in the term carbon constraints does not follow a narrow definition; it also covers other non-carbon-containing greenhouse gases as well as the direct negative effects of climate change (Lowe 2000; Hashimoto 2004; Busch and Hoffmann 2007; Hoffmann and Busch 2007). From a business standpoint, we define "constraints" as any sort of influence that limits the conditions by which firms conduct business and their efforts towards attaining profit. As such, carbon constraints are directly related to the profitability of corporate production processes and activities. This chapter examines the potential negative effects of carbon use in the industrial process along with its respective sources. How important it is for businesses to strive for low-carbon opportunities and generate competitive advantage through proactive climate change and carbon management strategies will be discussed in the third chapter.

Table 2 illustrates the general VITO (Vision, Inputs, Throughputs, and Outputs) view of sustainable organizations (Shrivastava 1995a, b). Following this view, organizations are entities that use carbon-based inputs and release carbon-containing outputs. The model also considers production processes that involve carbon conversions and transformations. As such, companies mediate the interface of the technosphere and ecosphere. On the input side are the fossil fuels in the natural environment (the ecosphere), which are transferred to an organization's production processes (the technosphere). After fossil fuels are used, carbon dioxide is emitted back to the atmosphere (ecosphere) (see Fig. 1). Thus, the input dimension of the model represents fossil fuels and fossil-fuel-based inputs, such as crude-oil-based plastics or coal-based electricity, while the output dimension refers to the emission of greenhouse gases in production processes, the most important part of which relates to carbon dioxide emissions. Other outputs include wastes and products, both of which contain carbon in some form. As these relations are affected by emerging carbon constraints, a closer examination of the sources of such constraints is necessary.

Table 2 **The VITO principles for sustainable organizations**

Source: Shrivastava 1995a, b

| Corporate elements | Environmental concerns | Positive potential |
|---|---|---|
| **Vision** | | |
| Self-identity | • Anthropocentrism<br>• Economic/ technological enterprise | • Social, ecological enterprise |
| Relationship to members | • Members as labor | • Concern for the whole person |
| Relationships with stakeholders | • Investors are primary stakeholders | • Multiple stakeholders plus nature |
| Relationships with nature | • Nature viewed as resource to be exploited | • Nature as a renewable resource |

| Corporate elements | Environmental concerns | Positive potential |
|---|---|---|
| **Inputs** | | |
| Raw materials | • Depletion of resources<br>• Harm caused by toxic materials | • Conservation<br>• Resource renewal<br>• User education |
| Fuels | • Fossil fuel depletion | • Conservation<br>• Efficiency |
| **Throughputs** | | |
| Plant | • Plant safety/ accidents<br>• Risks to neighborhoods<br>• Hazardous materials storage | • Liability insurance<br>• Eliminate bulk storage |
| Workers | • Occupational hazards<br>• Injuries/ill health | • Training in humane policies |
| Wastes | • Toxicity, disposal<br>• Pollution emissions | • Reduce, reuse, recycle<br>• Eliminate |
| Transportation | • Spills and losses | • Preventive measures |
| **Outputs** | | |
| Products | • Product safety<br>• Health consequences<br>• Product liability<br>• Environmental impacts | • Safer designs<br>• Product improvement<br>• User education<br>• Insurance<br>• Opportunities for environmentally friendly products |
| Packaging | • Garbage<br>• Reliability<br>• Pollution | • Recycle, reuse<br>• Design improvements<br>• Pollution control efficiency |

Figure 1 **Emerging carbon constraints for companies**

Source: Busch and Hoffmann 2007

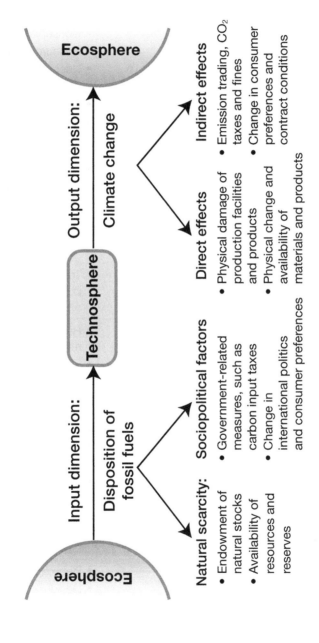

Earth's capacity to handle carbon transformations is complex and dynamic. Some carboniferous formations, such as oil and coal, took millions of years of fossilization. Carbon transformations such as plant life in the biosphere, on the other hand, occur on an annual or continuous basis. Others, such as animal life, have life cycles stretching to a few decades. The complex carbon systems on Earth have been studied and modeled by scientists, geographers, geologists, and ecologists for decades. Yet our understanding remains imperfect. In the business context, most companies have incorrectly assumed that energy and fossil fuels are sufficiently available at moderate prices, and that the emissions of greenhouse gases are free of charge. As their main objective is profit maximization, companies have not shown sufficient concern for carbon usage and emissions. However, some serious carbon-related changes are occurring in the business environment. For example, as new carbon and energy regulations are enforced, financial markets are exerting pressure on companies to disclose their climate change risks, illustrating that companies face new constraints.

Carbon constraints in terms of inputs are related to two aspects: natural scarcity of fossil fuels, and sociopolitical factors such as changing consumption patterns. Carbon constraints on the output side can be divided into direct and indirect climate change effects. The former describe direct physical impacts of climate change on a firm's assets and processes, and the latter encompass indirect impacts resulting from human efforts, such as climate policies directed towards mitigating climate change.

We will first focus on carbon constraints from the input dimension. To understand this, it is important to know how natural scarcity impacts market reactions. Resource scarcity is determined by several factors such as endowment of natural stocks, availability of resources and reserves, and technical developments. The expression "peak oil" has been quite pervasive in the discussion surrounding fossil fuel scarcity. The theory proposed by Hubbert (1956) describes the process of oil discovery and production as following a bell-shaped curve. The peak of this curve is described as the depletion mid-point, after which resources are said to be half depleted. We will describe this theory in more detail later in the book. The important point is:

once this peak has been acknowledged as an indication of emerging fossil fuel scarcity, markets start incorporating higher risk premiums and adjusting prices. Are we there yet? In 2008, there was a historic change in the International Energy Agency's forecast regarding future fossil fuel prices (see Chapter 4). The dramatic upwards adjustment of the predicted fossil fuel prices could be interpreted as an indication of emerging fossil fuel scarcity. For companies it is important to be aware that the resulting adjustments on energy markets will influence carbon input prices and constrain regular business functions, especially in carbon-intensive industries.

Beyond these potential effects stemming from natural scarcity, human factors such as government-related measures (e.g. taxes) and international political developments (particularly in oil-producing countries) may also cause price fluctuations. For example, in 1998 the German government introduced a stepwise carbon-input tax on petroleum and carbon-based electricity (renewable sources of energy are not taxed). Through this input tax, Germany was able to save 20 million tons of carbon dioxide in 2003, which represents approximately one-sixth of private household emissions (Knigge and Görlach 2005). Finland, Italy, Sweden, and the UK have also introduced carbon taxes since the 1990s. In the US, a carbon tax was first introduced in 2007 in Boulder, Colorado. With respect to non-governmental developments and the resulting carbon constraints, OPEC (Organization of the Petroleum Exporting Countries) is a powerful organization that is an important element in the (international) political realm of carbon constraints. After the fall in oil prices following an all-time peak in 2008, the organization implemented a cut in its production to stabilize prices. Without such measures, many oil-producing economies would face severe economic consequences (*The Economist* 2008). Such cuts and corresponding price mechanisms, however, have the same effect as any other regulation or intervention on markets; using carbon becomes more expensive.

Changes in consumer preferences are also important when considering carbon constraints in the input dimension: customers are becoming increasingly aware of the carbon footprint of their lifestyle. Consumption patterns will shift towards products that are less carbon-intensive in production and/or require less carbon during the usage phase. This in turn results in a carbon constraint for businesses: certain companies are not able to fulfill such demands for low-carbon products while their competitors are successfully able to do so. One of the most prominent examples is the growing demand for fuel-efficient cars. For instance, a psychological shift in fuel-efficiency awareness in consumers was seen when gasoline prices soared to $3 per gallon in the US. This increase in prices resulted in an immediate decline in driving distances. Although this effect was short-lived, it indicates the level and extent to which consumers are sensitive to varying prices of gasoline. Furthermore, this caused a long-lasting residual effect by shifting consumer preferences to fuel-efficient cars, thus impacting the auto industry. This trend is being seen in Europe and in the US where more consumers are considering fuel efficiency as a priority when deciding to purchase a new automobile.

Although there are examples for such consumer behavioral shifts, there still exists a profusion of conspicuous consumption supported by our media who valorize extreme affluence. There is now, however, a growing realization that consumption for the sake of consumption produces neither satisfaction nor happiness, and those excessive lifestyles may actually be drivers of diseases such as obesity, stress, and depression. Consumers are starting to question the veracity of advertising, the processes of need creation, and the issue of how much is "enough." Voluntary simplicity in lifestyle is a growing trend driven by processes of aging, consumption fatigue, and consumers who are becoming more skeptical of overconsumption (Johnston and Burton 2003).

Focusing now on carbon constraints on the output side, we will evaluate the direct and indirect effects of climate change. The former describes direct physical impacts of climate change on a company's assets and processes, such as damage to production facilities or availability of raw materials (e.g., water). The sources of these physical impacts are the steady changes in climate and increasing frequency and intensity of extreme weather events (IPCC 2007a). The steady changes in climate refers to increasing average ambient air and ocean temperatures, changes in precipitation, and rising sea levels. The increasing frequency and intensity of extreme weather

Figure 2 **Overall losses and insured losses: absolute values and long-term trends (1950–2008)**

Source: Munich Re NatCatSERVICE

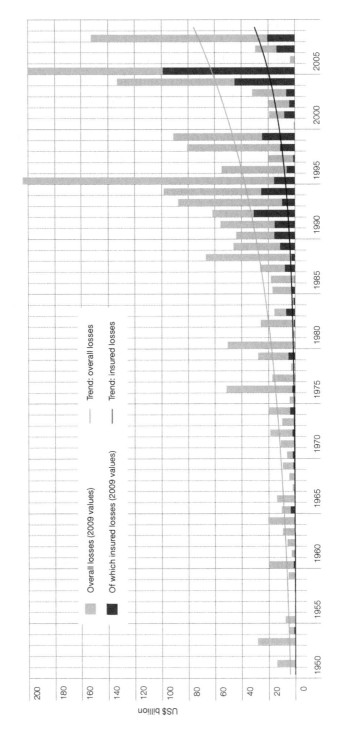

The chart presents the overall losses and insured losses – adjusted to present values. The trend curves document the increase in losses since 1950.

events refers to intense storms, extreme temperatures, increasing floods and droughts, and impacts on human health. As physical damages are usually insured, the resulting costs from damages by one massive event are of prime interest for insurance companies. Figure 2 illustrates how costs driven by damages arising from natural disasters have been steadily increasing in recent years.

With respect to the indirect effects of climate change, carbon constraints encompass governmental regulations, which are aimed at mitigating the effects of climate change. The most prominent example in this context is the European Emissions Trading Scheme. This scheme is an example of a market-based mechanism to reduce greenhouse gas emissions. It requires participating companies to render an emission allowance for each ton of carbon dioxide being emitted. If companies plan to emit more than the amount allocated, they must purchase additional allowances. Thus the pressure to reduce emissions will increase over time given the expected increases in the allowance price. We will comment on the current success of the system in the third part of the book.

Also, in the US, a potential cap-and-trade system is under debate and may come into force in the near future. Thus far, the Waxman-Markey bill (H.R. 2454: American Clean Energy and Security Act) has been the most ambitious cap-and-trade bill. It is also somewhat successful as it passed in the House in June 2009. The Kerry-Boxer bill (S. 1733) was also a cap-and-trade proposal targeted at emissions reductions by 20 percent by 2020 and 83 percent by 2050. However, it has been abandoned by Senator John Kerry, one of its sponsors, as he and Joe Lieberman are currently debating a new bill.

The last component of this dimension pertains to a firm's stakeholders, notably its consumers and financial market intermediaries (in addition to governments as discussed above). As previously discussed with respect to carbon-efficient products, consumption preferences have also shifted towards a greater climate consciousness. Many consumers and private households started buying "green" electricity or pro-climate labeled products such as those using the "ENERGY STAR."[1] Furthermore, corporate clients have increasingly demanded more detailed information about the emission charges

1  www.energystar.gov (accessed February 17, 2011).

of their supply chains. Companies within these supply chains are requested to report on their greenhouse gas emission levels and corporate strategies they use to curb emissions. The most prominent example to date is the initiative Walmart started in July 2009. The company intends to reduce the whole life cycle carbon footprint of its products, including its supply chain, by 20 million tons of carbon dioxide between 2010 and 2015 (Sturcken 2010). In order to do so, Walmart intends to rank its more than 100,000 suppliers based on a questionnaire (called a sustainability index). As a core component of the questionnaire the suppliers are asked for their levels of greenhouse gas emissions, corresponding reduction targets, and energy costs. Based on this information the company prioritizes products that may contribute to significant carbon reduction. The focus is laid on products with significant greenhouse gas emissions in their life cycle and top-selling items with potentially big carbon reduction potentials, such as clothing or pork. Such supply chain initiatives can be considered as the start of a huge transition process within industries. One must assume that the climate sensitivity of customers and business clients will continue to rise in the future and further contribute to this transition process.

With respect to financial market intermediaries, investors, insurance companies, and banks are becoming more actively engaged in assessing the climate change risks that companies are exposed to. Most notably, greater numbers of institutional investors are demanding more disclosure of data on emissions and related reduction strategies. Such demands include the necessity for clear statements of a company's emission reduction targets and implementation plans on company's carbon management practices. This development is also reflected in the growing scope of the Carbon Disclosure Project (CDP 2010), which currently queries more than 4,700 of the world's largest corporations for data on their greenhouse gas emissions, their climate risks, and carbon management strategies. The number of institutional investors supporting the project soared from 35 in 2003 (representing assets worth $4.5 trillion) to 534 in 2010 ($64 trillion worth of assets). As of 2010, 410 of the largest 500 global companies (based on market capitalization as in the FTSE Global Equity Index Series) have responded, a significant increase from 2003 when only

235 companies responded. Other examples of the pressures being placed on companies from this stakeholder group are the creation of the Dow Jones Sustainability Indexes, which have experienced a significant increase in investment volume since 2000,[2] and the global investor statement on climate change, which was released in November 2010 by almost 260 investors representing assets of over $15 trillion.[3] As decision makers consider such assessments and indices, more companies will be pushed towards a strategic consideration of their greenhouse gas emissions and respective reduction strategies. Furthermore, if risks continue to increase as a result of emerging carbon constraints, insurance companies will increase their premiums and/or reduce the coverage of environmental, technological, and disaster risks. Consequently, companies face different contract conditions, whereby they have to pay a risk premium for an increased risk exposure to carbon constraints. For instance, a recent study conducted by the Swiss Federal Institute of Technology (ETH) and the Swiss Reinsurance Company estimated that the mean increase in expected loss due to an increase in severity and frequency of storm events is 23 percent (10 years loss), 50 percent (30 years loss) and 104 percent (100 years loss) for Europe (Schwierz *et al.* 2009). Consequently, companies that operate in regions with a high exposure to storms or hurricanes bear this risk and face additional insurance premiums (Swiss Re 2006: 3):

> This means that the risk premium should reflect the changes in exposure, and the increased risk must be reflected in capital and capacity steering models. By doing so, insurers can determine with more accuracy individual risk and capital costs, and ensure that the allocated capacity and accompanying diversification more fully reflect the actual exposure.

Furthermore, in response to this increased exposure to weather-related losses, new insurance products are being developed. For example, event-linked futures are traded at the Insurance Futures

2 www.sam-group.com/htmle/djsi/indexes.cfm (accessed February 17, 2011).
3 www.unpri.org/files/Globalinvestorstatement.pdf (accessed March 14, 2011).

Exchange (IFEX) in Chicago.[4] Such future contracts provide a payment if (but only if) industry-wide losses from a specified natural catastrophe event reach a pre-specified loss level.

4 www.theifex.com/home (accessed February 17, 2011).

# 3
# Strategic benefits of carbon and climate strategies

Companies cannot treat carbon emissions as externalities any longer nor can they leave the solution to governments. It is in their own business's interest to strategize how to address carbon constraints and to understand their competitive implications. Following our VITO model of the firm, this chapter will discuss the strategic benefits of corporate carbon and climate strategies. When we view companies as a set of inputs, throughputs, and outputs, it is easy to see how the element carbon is intimately connected to virtually all company operations. Companies' strategies can focus on different angles, such as substituting its required inputs (fossil fuel, energy), optimizing the throughput system (greenhouse gas emissions stemming from operations, production, logistics), and the carbon-efficiency of its outputs (carbon intensity of products' usage). In each of these components, the implementation of carbon and climate strategies offers plenty of options for potential competitive advantage.

To start with, it is important that firms develop a clear *vision* expressing the commitment of the firm to establishing and living a low-carbon strategy. This is important since most companies' carbon constraints have not been outlined in their agenda. They historically treated energy as a utility good: that is, something that must be bought at the going rate from the local utility provider. However, with rising energy prices, and consumers' buying choices becoming more plentiful because of energy deregulation, companies can exercise greater discretion on energy procurement. In the past, the corporate contribution to climate change was not considered a strategic issue and emissions of greenhouse gases were taken for granted. As such, emerging carbon constraints should be reflected as a central part of a company's vision. Management should formulate energy and greenhouse gas emission goals and outline objectives towards designing a low-carbon product portfolio, one that relies less on fossil fuels and more on renewable energy sources.

From an *input* perspective, there is potential for enhancing overall corporate efficiencies and reducing fossil fuel use through the substitution of alternative energy sources. Today most production processes depend on fossil fuels (e.g., for heating purposes) and/or carbon-based materials (e.g., polymers) and electricity (e.g., coal-based); hence the decarbonization aspect of industrial technologies is very important. This requires substituting carbon-based inputs with renewable inputs. Most of the plastics we use today are produced from fossil-fuel-based polymers. The use of bio-polymers is still an exception, with no large-scale industrial applications. The same holds for electricity generation in industrialized countries. The prime energy source utilized today is coal, followed by natural gas. Only a few countries have pursued a clear low-carbon strategy in terms of investments in electricity generation power plants in recent years. For example, Switzerland's energy supply is composed of hydroelectricity (55%) and nuclear power (40%). Neglecting the negative impacts of nuclear power generation, especially in terms of contaminated waste, Switzerland presently has an almost carbon-free electricity mix. By extending and diversifying its renewable energy portfolio further with additional sources such as wind, biomass, photovoltaic, and thermo-solar, the country could now move towards a sustainable electricity mix.

*Throughput* systems or production/operation processes of companies can be another source of savings by attaining carbon efficiencies. For example, companies can reduce their greenhouse gas emissions by using cleaner production technologies with closed-loop systems and by being more mindful of resource consumption through recycling and reusing wastes. The Rocky Mountain Institute estimates that 75 percent of all energy produced in the US is wasted—a third in transmission losses, another third in energy inefficient devices, and the remainder due to poor usage habits. In almost every company there are possibilities for cutting costs and improving profitability by using energy-efficient devices such as motors, refrigerators, coolers, and air conditioners. For example, commercial energy contracts that produce energy in one state, such as California, and sell it to another state, such as Maine, create unnecessary waste. Rationalizing these energy contracts can offer huge savings for utility companies. In addition, logistics and transportation-intensive companies should investigate options for more efficient transportation systems. Lastly, there are plenty of opportunities to increase carbon efficiency in any firm relating to human resources: employee work spaces, transportation for work-related meetings, commuting to work, employee food, and so on. With these actions, companies can improve their ecological performance, reduce their costs, minimize their liabilities and risk exposure, all while improving their corporate image and increasing their revenues.

Corporate *outputs* in the form of products and wastes are also ripe for sourcing carbon efficiencies and generating a competitive advantage. Energy-dependent products can be designed in an energy-efficient manner by making them less costly and less carbon-intensive to operate. This is an important consideration given that consumers are becoming increasingly aware of the carbon footprints of the products they purchase. Furthermore, with rising costs of fossil fuels and energy, the carbon efficiency of products in their use phase also determines consumers' purchasing decisions. This requires adequate communication, for example, as is the case with the energy-efficiency labels that consumers can find on laundry and dish washers.

Today, policy makers and corporate leaders are increasingly aware of the need to increase their efforts to establish a "low-carbon economy." The effectiveness of current policy efforts on the international level will be addressed in the third part of the book. For the corporate dimension, the idea that carbon is a fundamental driver of costs and revenues is a revolutionary concept. In light of the problems posed by global carbon accumulation and their sources in corporate activities, a necessary first step for companies is to take a strategic approach. In order to start thinking strategically about the carbon challenges in the input, throughput, and output dimension companies must realize the emerging institutional environment of carbon, in which they are embedded. There has been an extensive amount of scientific research for nearly a quarter-century on the topic of climate change caused by carbon accumulation. While our scientific understanding is still evolving on certain aspects, as the second part of the book discusses in more detail, the policy environment (both domestic and international) has changed dramatically. For the past twenty years, Earth Summits and various international treaties (Rio to Kyoto to Cancun) have shaped the political landscape and intensified the discussion about sustainable development and climate change. Although we have to critically reflect on recent climate policy developments at the international level, we should also acknowledge that much has been achieved and that governments still seek to establish a new (post-Kyoto) climate treaty. Beyond that there is a strong indication that many countries individually intend to implement new climate and energy regulation, which in some cases will affect virtually every industry sector. Moreover, public opinion on the issue of climate change has fragmented into multiple voices. Oftentimes, these voices are in conflict with one another, each striving for more attention than the other. Nevertheless, there is a clear indication that consumers, customers, and employees—all important stakeholders of a firm—are aware of climate change and energy security as pressing issues. This forms their values and beliefs, which in turn affect their daily life decisions—organizational scientists call this social movement, a development that is certainly on the rise.

In general, it should be an imperative for companies to engage strategically with carbon and climate challenges. The recent BP accident in the Gulf of Mexico—which is also interesting in the broader carbon context as BP's main business is extracting crude oil and selling gas and diesel to customers—illustrates the devastating consequences for a firm when important principles with respect to the natural environment are neglected. The carbon crisis is now emerging at a time when the world is already reeling from another crisis— the global financial crisis triggered in late 2008. Within a year the financial crisis had engulfed all major economies of the world. As of 2009, for the first time since World War II, the world economy was set to shrink rather than grow. The estimated cost of stabilizing the world financial markets and stimulating economies back into growth is said to be over five trillion dollars. Representing a large amount of money to be put back into the global economy, there are two ways in which firms may use this money. The first is in a carbon-insensitive manner: that is, firms just revive old patterns of production and consumption. The other is by moving the world toward renewable energy regimes, and sustainable consumption and production in order to positively impact or even prevent a global carbon crisis.

Strategic management of carbon issues will require long-term investments, which will add new metrics to measure the sustainability of investments beyond the commonly used financial metrics such as return on investment and net present value analysis. These new metrics can follow three complementary strategies (Huber 2000):

1. **Efficiency strategy.** Companies should seek to reduce their use of fossil fuels and decrease their greenhouse gas emissions per output. This can be achieved via increased energy and carbon efficiency and substitution of fossil fuels. As previously mentioned for the macro level, firms are also required to follow the decoupling and decarbonization logic in terms of their energy investments in order to contribute to a low-carbon society

2. **Consistency strategy.** Firms should target long-term investments that have underlying carbon and energy flows compatible with ecological systems. The human use of carbon should not interfere negatively with the cycles of the natural environment. In other words, we must be conscious of the limitations of our natural environment to absorb carbon. As we are already above this limit and still putting more and more greenhouse gases into the atmosphere, the greenhouse

effect will further accelerate. We need to limit carbon emissions in the same range as the ecological capacity to reabsorb that carbon

3. **Sufficiency strategy.** Businesses and humankind need to understand that unlimited economic growth under current ecological conditions is not possible. Through changing lifestyles, every individual can contribute to significant carbon throughput reductions. For firms this entails focusing on creating long-lasting and easy-to-repair products and developing unique low-carbon service strategies. The main objective is still to fulfill reasonable consumer needs, but to significantly reduce the required material, energy, and carbon flows

By acknowledging these three complementary strategies first suggested by Huber (2000) in the broader sustainability context, firms work towards reaping carbon efficiencies and establishing new business models. Long-term investment strategies will steer firms in this direction, thereby allowing them to prosper in a carbon-constrained business environment. Internally, companies will need to adopt appropriate strategies in their product designs, production systems, transportation and logistics, natural and human resource management. Such strategies allow companies to deal with long-term, system-wide challenges in a manner that gives them a competitive advantage. So while the carbon challenge may be a source of crisis (if it is not addressed) it can also be a source of opportunity if companies adopt a strategic perspective that encourages proactive change. Identifying decision choices, thinking about decision criteria, setting goals, and deliberately managing carbon footprints can help companies achieve this. Such measures will allow companies to make changes before public pressures and government regulation narrow the range of options available.

In summary, our elaborations and discussions demonstrate the systemic connections between firms and the multifaceted element carbon. For companies, the use of carbon and its consequences have moved from being a disregarded "externality" issue to becoming a strategic variable that can be a source of competitive advantage, an element of product quality, and a key ingredient to gain legitimacy in society. Understanding the connection between business operations and the resulting carbon footprint is a good first step for building carbon-based competitive advantage. Based on this, further steps can follow: reducing one's own carbon footprint, trading carbon credits, and/or building carbon efficiencies into product design and production systems. The third part of this book will reexamine this topic and discuss a proactive carbon management framework, which companies may use on their path towards this end.

# Part II

# The carbon crisis: physical science, economic, and equity perspectives

# 4
# Evolution of carbon utilization

Carbon is the basic element that constitutes life. The abundance of carbon compounds is possible because of its ability to form strong covalent (chemical) bonds with many elements, particularly oxygen, hydrogen, and metals. Carbon atoms have the special property of bonding with each other forming chains, rings, spheres, and tubes; chains of carbon atoms can be thousands of atoms long. This chapter discusses the sources of the global carbon crisis from a physical science point of view, focusing on the input dimension of emerging carbon constraints. We will focus on the intensification of carbon utilization and the consequences arising from natural availability limits.

## Natural fossil fuel availability

Our discussion regarding emerging carbon constraints has emphasized that the emission of carbon in terms of carbon dioxide is a problem for society and creates constraints for businesses (output dimension). We have also acknowledged that the limited availability of carbon in terms of fossil fuels poses a serious constraint for industry (input dimension). With a fixed quantity of carbon locked in the form of crude oil, oil sands, coal, and gas on the planet and with the current technologies of extraction and refining, it is only a matter of time before we reach the natural limits. Humans have always had a carbon footprint, but the amount of human carbon utilization has increased significantly over time, especially since the industrial revolution. There has been a significant acceleration in the way we utilize the naturally limited fossil fuel reserves of our planet. Realizing that natural fossil fuel availability is not a "bottomless pit" becomes particularly important when taking into account anticipated future fossil fuel consumption: the global demand for all types of fossil fuel is predicted to rise constantly over the next two decades (see Table 3), which can mainly be ascribed to a sharp rise in demand from newly industrializing countries (Mabey and Mitchell 2010).

Table 3 **World primary energy demand by fossil fuel (per annum; 2015 and 2030 predicted demand by IEA reference scenario), in million tons of oil equivalent (Mtoe)**

Source: IEA 2008

|       | 1980  | 2000  | 2006  | 2015  | 2030  | 2006–2030* |
|-------|-------|-------|-------|-------|-------|------------|
| Coal  | 1,788 | 2,295 | 3,053 | 4,023 | 4,908 | 2.0%       |
| Oil   | 3,107 | 3,649 | 4,029 | 4,525 | 5,109 | 1.0%       |
| Gas   | 1,235 | 2,088 | 2,407 | 2,903 | 3,670 | 1.8%       |

* Average annual rate of growth

We illustrate the limits of this current "bottomless pit" understanding by referring to the example of crude oil. The data reported in Table 3 gives exact numbers for the *ex post* consumption. Adding all these numbers up yields the so-called global cumulative production, which was about 1,128 billion barrels in 2007 (Sorrell *et al.* 2010). For investigating where we are in terms of the depletion rate, the cumulative production needs to be compared with estimates for proven reserves of crude oil. Various organizations compile and report data on proved oil reserves. These reports use different estimation methods and data sources and are based on different assumptions, such as exploitation rates. Consequently, the different reports yield different results. In 2009 the Energy Information Administration summarized the results from some important sources of such estimates (Table 4). Taking into account the result for global cumulative production, we can roughly say that, since the beginnings of industrialization up to today, half of the oil reserves have already been used. How long will the second half last?

Table 4 **Most recent estimates for world proved reserves of crude oil, in billion barrels of oil**

Source: Energy Information Administration, www.eia.doe.gov/emeu/international/oilreserves.html (accessed February 18, 2011)

| Oil reserves (estimates) | Source | Reference date |
|---|---|---|
| 1,184 | World Oil | Year-end 2007 |
| 1,239 | BP Statistical Review | Year-end 2007 |
| 1,342 | *Oil & Gas Journal* | January 1, 2009 |

Many studies are concerned with this question and have sought to give an answer. A recent report conducted by the UK Energy Research Centre (Sorrell *et al*. 2009) reviewed more than 500 studies and concluded that the studies vary widely regarding their theoretical basis, inclusion of variables, and level of aggregation and complexity. As each approach has certain strengths and weaknesses, we do not want to go further into the details and, instead, perform a very simple calculation based on the data sources provided in Table 4. Let us assume that there were 1,200 billion barrels of proven oil reserves left at the end of 2007. This corresponds to 164 billion tons (7.3 barrels per ton). Let us further assume that there will be an annual global oil demand as predicted by the official IEA forecasts (see Table 3). In 2006 the annual oil consumption was about 4,029 million tons. Taking into account the predicted 1 percent annual growth in consumption, this brings us right to the year 2040, where the cumulative consumption hits the threshold of 164 billion tons and the point of final depletion is reached. This leaves us approximately 30 years until the last barrel is gone. A very gloomy picture of the future, notably when one considers the high carbon dependency of the current production system. However, is this also the time left until oil scarcity will eventually merge? The answer is no: resource scarcity emerges through markets and the time when markets start pricing scarcity for individual fossil fuels depends on several factors.

## Emerging fossil fuel scarcity

Resource scarcity is determined by several factors such as endowment of natural stocks, availability of resources, new discoveries, and technological and economic developments. We discussed earlier that oil discovery and production can be explained as a bell-shaped curve with depletion mid-point as the point in time that oil production starts to decline (Hubbert 1956). In 1956 Hubbert predicted that oil production in the US would peak between 1965 and 1972. In fact it peaked in 1970 (Stoft 2008). Although, in theory, the production peak-point and depletion mid-point should coincide, this is not always the case given that production can be held up (or even increased) artificially for a few years through technical interference or quota regulation. However, once it has been recognized that natural scarcity is an emerging issue in the long-term, this will prompt markets to incorporate higher risk premiums and will result in an adjustment of prices. According to geologist Kenneth S. Deffeyes (2005), one of the more recent peak-oil theorists, the most worrying time is the five-year window after the peak. For this window Deffeyes expects a steep decline in oil production and the most severe economic consequences.

The Association for the Study of Peak Oil and Gas (ASPO), an international group founded by geologist Colin Campbell, regularly estimates the availability of fossil fuels. Figure 3 shows estimates for the global production of oil and gas by this group. The graph shows the cumulative global oil and gas production measured in giga barrels of oil equivalent. What can be seen is that the cumulative global oil and gas production was said to peak in 2008. Considering individual fossil fuels, ASPO estimates that crude oil peaked in 2005 and gas

Figure 3 **Oil and gas production profiles: 2008 base case**

Source: Colin Campbell and www.peakoil.net (accessed February 18, 2011)

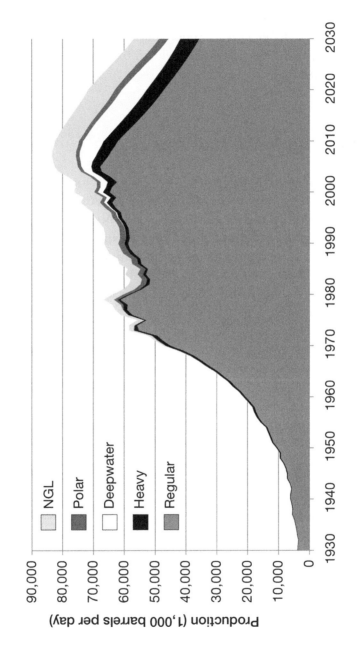

liquid is about to peak in 2020 (ASPO 2009). Other studies are more optimistic about the peak oil date. For example, Sorrell *et al.* (2010: 5,294) suggest that the "peak of conventional oil production before 2030 appears likely and there is a significant risk of a peak before 2020." The authors propose that the methodologies frequently lead to underestimates of the proven resources and overly pessimistic forecasts regarding future supply (Sorrell *et al.* 2009).

However, the main question is not when the peak of crude oil and other fossil fuels actually will take place, or has already happened, as ASPO would argue for oil. From a business perspective it is more important how markets reflect emerging scarcity and notably the fear of future scarcity. Such reflections not only determine the price level for fossil fuels but also affect price volatilities (Hirsch *et al.* 2005; Lovins *et al.* 2005). This means that there is no longer a stable price level, and that prices will fluctuate constantly. Arbitrary fluctuations impede accurate investment planning, as the profitability and amortization periods cannot be calculated in a precise and reliable manner. For companies it is therefore important to be aware that the scarcity-induced adjustment processes on energy markets will influence carbon input prices and constrain companies in their way of doing business, especially in highly carbon-intense industries. The future availability of fossil fuels and related price developments must be considered as important sources of uncertainty and cost escalation. This is already of rising concern for many governments and companies (e.g., ITPOES 2010; Mabey and Mitchell 2010).

# Carbon scarcity skeptics

Critics may consider the ASPO estimates as being too pessimistic, arguing that mankind and industry need not worry about fossil fuel scarcity. They argue that—at least in their own time horizon—there always has been oil and thus there always will be oil. In case extraction ends in certain areas, new oil fields will be discovered and new technical developments will enable the use of different reserves (such as oil sands) and extension of the exploitation limits of existing oil fields. Others, coming more from an economic point of view, argue that even increasing fossil fuel prices are no reason to worry. In such a case, alternative technologies based on renewable energy sources will become financially competitive and they thus will substitute fossil-fuel-based technologies. However, there is a broad consensus that such required developments—in terms of new oil extraction as well as renewable technologies—take time. Such technologies first have to mature and their global diffusion will not take place instantaneously. Taking into account that the currently established production and consumption patterns are highly fossil-fuel-dependent and the demand for oil in emerging economies such as China and India is growing rapidly, increasing fossil fuel scarcity must be considered an important constraint on economic development.

As a response, many governments of industrialized countries are becoming increasingly concerned about the high oil dependency of their economies. With the disruption in oil supplies in 1973 and a (thus far) all-time high in the price of crude oil in 2008, these governments fear that similar developments may interfere in their future prosperity and economic development. Evidence that justifies this fear can be seen by looking at the 2008 historic changes of fossil fuel price predictions by the International Energy Agency's (IEA 2008) *World Energy Outlook* (see Table 5). Before this report, the yearly published forecasts seemed to deny the fact that emerging fossil fuel scarcity would affect prices, as can be seen in the moderate price projections up to 2030. For example, in the 2006 report it was assumed that in 2030 one barrel of crude oil would be about $55 (accounting for inflation, i.e. in 2005 prices). However, when comparing this with the 2008 report one can see a dramatic change in the agency's forecast regarding future fossil fuel prices. The same barrel that was estimated to be $55 changed to about $122. This is an increase of about 114 percent. As such, evidence from the IEA indicates that a development towards a more carbon-constrained business environment is imminent.

Table 5 **IEA's historic change in fossil fuel prices forecasts**

Source: Price estimates in the Reference Scenario (IEA 2006, 2008)

| | Unit | World Energy Outlook 2006 | World Energy Outlook 2008 | Change 2006–2008 estimate |
|---|---|---|---|---|
| **Crude oil (IEA) 2010** | | | | |
| Real | Per barrel | US$52 (2005) | US$100 (2007) | |
| Nominal | Per barrel | US$58 | US$107 | +84% |
| **Crude oil (IEA) 2030** | | | | |
| Real | Per barrel | US$55 (2005) | US$122 (2007) | |
| Nominal | Per barrel | US$97 | US$206 | +114% |
| **Natural gas (US) 2010** | | | | |
| Real | Per Mbtu | US$6.67 (2005) | US$12.78 (2007) | |
| Nominal | Per Mbtu | US$7.49 | US$13.72 | +83% |
| **Natural gas (US) 2030** | | | | |
| Real | Per Mbtu | US$6.92 (2005) | US$16.13 (2007) | |
| Nominal | Per Mbtu | US$12.24 | US$27.28 | +123% |
| **Steam coal (OECD) 2010** | | | | |
| Real | Per tonne | US$55 (2005) | US$120 (2007) | |
| Nominal | Per tonne | US$62 | US$129 | +108% |
| **Steam coal (OECD) 2030** | | | | |
| Real | Per tonne | US$60 (2005) | US$110 (2007) | |
| Nominal | Per tonne | US$106 | US$186 | +75% |

For almost every theory that seeks to predict future developments there exists some form of theoretical and/or empirical academic support. To this end, support of a certain side of a debate regarding future developments is a function of one's beliefs, which is influenced by how convincing and trustworthy arguments are articulated, and one's perception regarding which assumptions seem to most adequately reflect reality. With fossil fuel scarcity, however, the story is slightly different. Although this issue also deals with one's beliefs, these are beliefs that represent market participants: if scarcity is considered to be relevant then prices will go up—this is independent of whether there is convincing academic support for peak oil to be a reality or not. This, for example, can also be triggered by political developments or strategic interests. In this context, the function and unpredictable strategies of OPEC play an important role (cf. Stoft 2008): this cartel's decisions on production capacities determine whether unusual price developments in markets will accelerate or will flatten. Furthermore, it is important to note that market participants and their expectations are influenced by non-rational facts, psychological effects and herd behavior, which results in behaviors that often defy what would be predicted from a purely rational perspective. These factors therefore make it difficult to predict exactly when and how markets will react to declining fossil fuels. However, one thing is certain: markets will react to this reality once they realize that scarcity is actually emerging and this in turn will impose a definite constraint on the business environment.

# 5
# Climate change challenges ahead

While the previous chapter took a look at the input dimension, this chapter focuses on the output dimension: climate change. Such a comprehensive view on both dimensions is important when discussing the consequences of the global carbon crisis for businesses— carbon constraints emerge and need to be addressed on the in- and output side.

## Increasing levels of greenhouse gases

Compared with the actual utilization of carbon and carbon-based materials, for example for cooking, our appreciation of carbon emissions and their role within the natural environment is even more recent—dating back to the 1950s. Scientists have been studying ice cores and isotopic composition of plants, in an effort to understand the presence and role of carbon in ancient climates. The concentration of carbon dioxide in the atmosphere has significantly increased since the beginning of the industrial revolution. Just between 1970 and 2004 annual emissions have grown by about 80 percent, from 21 to 38 gigatons (IPCC 2007b). Presently, global carbon dioxide emissions continue to rise because of a lack of far-reaching changes that are needed in the core processes of industrialization, consumption, and human habitat.

When discussing the sources of climate change, one must also consider important elements other than carbon dioxide ($CO_2$). The Intergovernmental Panel on Climate Change (IPCC) has agreed on six gases which, through intensified anthropogenic use and release, are responsible for accelerated climate change: carbon dioxide, methane, nitrous oxide, hydrofluorocarbons, perfluorocarbons, and sulfur hexafluoride. All six gases are usually measured according to their global warming potential in $CO_2$-equivalents. Nevertheless, carbon dioxide is the most important anthropogenic greenhouse gas: for example, in 2004 it represented 77 percent of the total greenhouse gas emissions (IPCC 2007b).

Greenhouse gases in the atmosphere have remained nearly constant from the beginning of civilization 10,000 BCE to the beginning of the industrial revolution. Estimates by the IPCC (2007c) show that carbon dioxide has hovered around 270 to 280 parts per million (compare Figure 4). By 2008, however, this level had increased to 387 parts per million, which represents an increase of about 40 percent. The increase is caused by human activities and can be ascribed to two main developments. First, a large percentage of atmospheric carbon dioxide concentrations come from and will continue to come from the use of fossil fuels (coal, oil, and natural gas) for energy. Carbon dioxide emissions from fossil-fuel burning and industrial processes have been accelerating at a global scale: between 1990 and 1999 there was an annual growth rate of about 1 percent; for the period 2000 to 2004 the rate was larger than 3 percent (Raupach *et al.* 2007). Second, about a quarter of the increase over the last 150 years has come from changes in land use: for example, the clearing of forests and the cultivation of soils for food production. Thus, deforestation has significantly contributed to an increasing carbon dioxide concentration in the atmosphere: as the number of trees has been reduced, the capacity of our planet to absorb carbon dioxide has also been diminished. Furthermore, burning of forests has been shown to release previously captured carbon dioxide back into the atmosphere. Figure 4 illustrates a similar development (increase in concentration) for two other IPCC greenhouse gases, methane and nitrous oxide.

Figure 4  **Increasing accumulation of greenhouse gases (AD 0–2005)**

Source: IPCC 2007c: Frequently Asked Questions, Figure 1

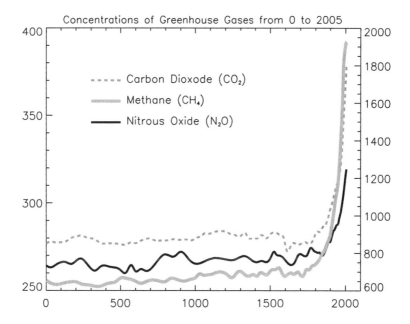

# Sources of climatic changes

The global climate evolves over time owing to naturally occurring factors outside the climate system such as volcanic eruptions and solar variations. However, in recent years this climate evolution has become more marked as a result of human activities, which have induced changes in the atmosphere's composition. The majority of serious climate scientists ascribe the unprecedented increase in recent concentrations of greenhouse gases to human activities, especially the burning of fossil fuels and deforestation (Sills 2010). Reports published by the IPCC (2007b) and Stern (2006) outline the effects of the increasing accumulation of anthropogenic greenhouse gases on the Earth's climate system. The main consequences can be summarized as follows.

The sun is ultimately the source of virtually all energy that reaches the Earth's surface. The Earth receives and absorbs solar energy, which is then either reflected or radiated back out into space. This highly complex balance between reception, absorption, and emission can, however, be upset by several factors (Lashof 1989): by a change in the amount of incoming radiation (i.e., through changes in the Earth's orbit around the sun); by a change in the amount of radiation that is reflected back due to an increase in atmospheric particles, such as through volcanic activity or differing levels of cloud cover; and by changes in the amount of long-wave radiation emitted by the planet back out into space, which can occur as a consequence of changing greenhouse gas concentrations. Assuming stable conditions, that is, a constant average temperature over time, one can argue that the total amount of energy entering the Earth's system from solar radiation as well as the amount being radiated into space should not change. In sum, it is important to be aware that the greenhouse effect is necessary; without it the amount of solar energy reaching the Earth's surface would result in average temperatures being way below freezing point. Essentially, the temperatures we are familiar with can be attributed to the absorption process of greenhouse gases by which energy is captured in the atmosphere to warm the Earth's surface.

Through these processes, the increase in greenhouse gas concentrations since the beginning of industrialization has already caused the planet to warm by over half a degree Celsius. Even in the absence of further emission increases it is estimated that there will be "at least a further half a degree warming over the next few decades, because of the inertia in the climate system" (Stern 2006: 3). As consequence, the fourth assessment report of the IPCC emphasizes that in the long-term further climate change is unequivocal. Although different models, which use different assumptions, will naturally yield different results, the business as usual assumptions provided by the

IPCC scenarios in Figure 5 show almost no estimate falling below an expected temperature increase of two degrees; only one optimistic scenario (B1) is just below the two degrees mark.

Figure 5 **IPCC scenarios for temperature anomaly**

Source: IPCC 2007c: Summary for Policymakers, Figure SPM.5

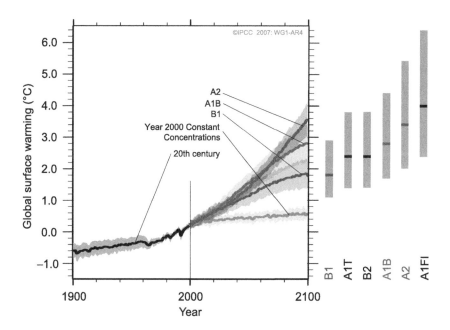

Solid lines are multi-model global averages of surface warming (relative to 1980–1999) for the scenarios A2, A1B and B1, shown as continuations of the 20th-century simulations. Shading denotes the ±1 standard deviation range of individual model annual averages. The line on the bottom of the right half is for the experiment where concentrations were held constant at year 2000 values. The gray bars on the right indicate the best estimate (solid line within each bar) and the likely range assessed for six scenarios

# Incorporating feedback mechanisms

We discussed anthropogenic greenhouse gases as the main source of climate change, of which one central consequence is global warming.

Having started this process, the warming of the planet then reinforces itself. Such phenomena are known as feedback mechanisms, which are important because they play a crucial role within the climate system. Feedbacks are second-order effects that can amplify or dampen a given primary effect. On the one hand, there is the $CO_2$ fertilization effect: as more $CO_2$ becomes available for plants, there is increased vegetation growth which dampens $CO_2$ accumulation. On the other hand, there are a couple of effects that further amplify climate change, which in sum outweigh the dampening effect. The prime example is the effect of reduced natural reflection. With increasing temperatures, snow and ice begin to melt and the darker surfaces beneath are revealed. These darker surfaces reflect less radiation back into space. A feedback loop is initiated, which warms the planet further, and thus drives more melting. This feedback loop is known as the "ice-albedo feedback."

Another example is the diminishing capacity of nature to serve as a natural carbon sink. A large part of the anthropogenic emissions of carbon dioxide ends up in the Earth's oceans, but as oceans warm they can hold less carbon dioxide. Thus global warming and the subsequent increase in ocean temperatures will add to carbon in the atmosphere and deprive the world of a valuable carbon sink, thereby contributing further to climate change. In a similar manner the Arctic is another important carbon sink. In the low temperatures of the Arctic much plant matter does not decompose, and therefore carbon accumulates in the soil. It has been estimated that the land in the Arctic holds roughly a third of all carbon contained in terrestrial ecosystems globally. However with global warming causing the Arctic to melt this can only add to the vicious cycle, by further contributing to climate change. The same arguments can be made for the large areas of permafrost that are melting; permafrost is another important carbon sink as it locks in significant amounts of methane.

Water vapor represents another important feedback mechanism. Direct emission of water vapor by human activities makes a negligible contribution to climate change, i.e. it does not result in a significant change in the balance of incoming and outgoing energy in the Earth–atmosphere system. However, with global average temperatures increasing, tropospheric water vapor concentrations also increase. As water vapor is an important natural greenhouse gas, such changing water vapor concentrations result in a feedback loop affecting the equilibrium of climate sensitivity and can further accelerate climate change.

While feedback through the terrestrial and oceanic uptake of atmospheric carbon dioxide and other effects may further contribute to climate change for a given emissions scenario, the exact strength of different feedback effects varies markedly among models. Nevertheless, based on this discussion regarding feedback mechanisms, it becomes clear that climate change is not a linear and fully predictable process. Most of the occurring feedback mechanisms further accelerate climate change. As such, the future change in the climate itself and the resulting consequences for ecosystems, human beings, and businesses are subject to uncertainties.

## Climate variability

The IPPC (2007c) research considers the global climate as having been relatively stable in the last 2,000 years before 1850, with regional fluctuations (see Fig. 6). The two most famous fluctuations are labeled the Medieval Warm Period (*c*. AD 1000–1250) and the Little Ice Age (*c*. AD 1550–1850) . These two periods have often been invoked in discussions of global warming; critics of the theory of human-induced climate change use these examples to demonstrate that there always has been a certain degree of climate variability. However, what these critics fail to recognize is that these fluctuations have been regional and were not related to changing concentrations of greenhouse gases in the atmosphere. The timing of the cold and warm periods has been demonstrated to vary geographically and chronologically across the globe.

The IPCC (2001) cites several estimates for the northern hemisphere's mean temperatures which indicate that temperatures from the 11th to the 14th centuries were approximately 0.2 degrees Celsius warmer than from the 15th to 19th centuries. However, these higher temperatures in the so-called Medieval Warm Period were still below those found in the mid-20th century. Regional evidence

Figure 6 **Historical developments of climatic changes**

Source: IPCC 2007c: Technical Summary, Figure TS.20

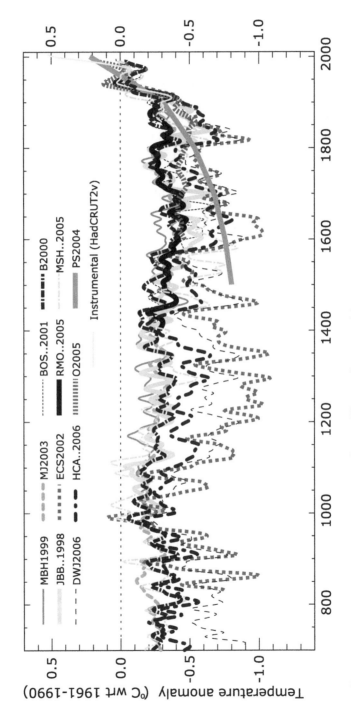

Different colors represent measurements according to different climate models

is quite variable. For example, in the southern hemisphere some studies found no evidence for a distinct Medieval Warm Period (e.g., Crowley and Lowery 2000), while others suggest that at least part of the warming was global (Broecker 2001; Keigwin 1996). This medieval warmth in the North Atlantic and neighboring areas was followed by a cooler period, with temperatures dropping by about 0.6 degrees Celsius during the 15th and 19th centuries (Mann 2002). The Little Ice Age appears to have been most clearly expressed in the North Atlantic region as altered patterns of atmospheric circulation. Central Europe experienced unusually cold, dry winters; temperatures were one to two degrees Celsius below normal during the late 17th century (IPCC 2001). Literature suggests that these cold winters could be ascribed to more frequent flows of continental air from the north-east (e.g., Alcoforado *et al.* 2000). Although the evidence for temperature changes in past centuries in the southern hemisphere is quite sparse, the IPCC (2001) concludes that there appeared to have been marked differences compared with the northern hemisphere.

Research on both of these phenomena has pointed to the role of ocean circulation-related climate variability (Broecker 2001). Temperature changes in the Atlantic region may reflect century-scale changes in the North Atlantic oscillation (Keigwin and Pickart 1999). Such regional changes in oceanic and atmospheric processes have had primary regional effects. In a similar manner the El Niño phenomenon is thought to have had the main influence on *regional* temperature patterns over North America (IPCC 2001). The sources of such variability may be difficult to understand, however. Nevertheless, it is obvious that this variability cannot be ascribed to huge variations in the level of greenhouse gases. As such, it is impossible to compare and discuss the Medieval Warm Period and the Little Ice Age with what is being experienced in the current warming phenomenon. In other words, although there is empirical evidence for natural climate variability (Keigwin 1996), such climatic changes in the past were nearly independent of variations in the concentration of greenhouse gases. The source of the current climate variability is a significant increase in greenhouse gases concentrations that we have not experienced thus far—as such humankind is facing a very different development compared with past changes of the climate.

# Changing natural environment due to climate change

The natural environment has already experienced significant changes as a result of climate change. This can be observed directly on a global scale in the decline of snow and ice cover over many years, especially since the 1980s and increasingly during the past decade (IPCC 2007b). Sea ice has declined and is becoming thinner as indicated by satellite data, surface waters of the Arctic Ocean have warmed, and in some areas permafrost is rapidly thawing. This can be illustrated by a recent report published by the Arctic Monitoring and Assessment Programme (AMAP 2009): in 2007, some parts of the Arctic Ocean were as much as five degrees warmer than the long-term average as a result of an influx of warmer water from the Pacific and Atlantic. Arctic sea ice levels were recorded to be at their lowest point in the winter of 2008. There has also been significant thinning due to loss of perennial ice, which has been decreasing since 1957, and the thinning ice is becoming even more susceptible to melting. In Greenland, the summer temperatures have been consistently above the long-term average since the mid-1990s. In 2007 the annual melt was 60 percent larger than in 1998. It has also been estimated that overall snow cover in the northern hemisphere has been declining by about 1 to 2 percent per year and glaciers have been shrinking at an incredibly fast pace. The report highlights that, for the first time since records have been kept, both the north-west and north-east passages were free of ice in 2008 (AMAP 2009).

Increasing temperatures and changing weather patterns already affect biodiversity and cause plants and trees to grow more vigorously, particularly in Arctic tundra areas. In some areas of Russia, for example, the tree line has advanced up hills and mountains by as much as 10 meters per year (AMAP 2009). Satellite observations since the early 1980s are showing an early "greening" pattern of vegetation in the spring, which is linked to longer thermal growing seasons. In addition, shifts in ranges and quantities of algae, plankton, and fish in oceans, lakes, and rivers are being experienced. Furthermore, rising water temperatures and changes in ice cover, salinity, oxygen levels, and circulation affect the marine and freshwater biological systems. While some of the discussed effects may not be interpreted as a negative consequence yet, in other areas climate change has already had negative impacts. For example, many experts predict that Africa will be affected the most by climate change and is already experiencing negative consequences (Bloomfield 2006): owing to the warming experienced in the 20th century, rainfall has decreased in the Sahel region by 25 percent in the last 30 years. As a consequence, local agriculture has been affected and cereal crop yields have been falling. Africa's tropical rainforests have also witnessed a significant fall in precipitation since the mid-1970s. Furthermore, droughts in the Sahel and the Horn of Africa have become more regular since the 1960s (Bloomfield 2006).

Next to these already tangible effects, climate change will further affect natural and human environments in future. Some of these effects can only be predicted with slight confidence, others are difficult to discern because of successful adaptation efforts and non-climatic drivers. Without emphasizing too many details, we concentrate on summarizing the likely consequences for weather patterns, the global water system, natural ecosystems, agriculture, and human systems.

The predicted climatic variations will change **weather patterns**, which will become most obvious in the form of increases in extreme weather events, such as hurricanes and heat waves. Although there is evidence that this is already occurring, some extreme weather events are likely to increase further in severity with further climatic changes. Considering the steady increase of average temperatures, climate change will cause variations in regional weather systems. These effects of climate change will be magnified for developing nations, where climates tend to be drier and warmer on average than developed countries, and because many of these regions already experience a high level of rainfall variability. To add to this, developing countries, more than other nations, rely heavily on agriculture as their main source of income, an activity that depends on appropriate climatic conditions. Owing to a generally lower level of national income provisions, financial resources are limited, and as such the ability to adapt to climate change is constrained. Therefore, it can be expected that changing weather patterns will hit poor countries such as African nations the most (Bloomfield 2006).

Climate change also holds implications for the **global water system**. For example, melting glaciers will result in two opposing effects, depending on the time horizon. In the short run, there will be increased flood risks as the water systems in the valleys may exceed their absorption capacities because of the additional water. In the long run, once the ice is melted, there will be reductions in the water supply. Especially in hot and dry summers the lack of this additional water source will disrupt the water systems in the valleys and may even result in dried-out rivers (IPCC 2007b). This will become an issue in many parts of the world, for example India and China. In addition, there is an expected growth in ground instability in permafrost regions and increased frequency of rock avalanches in mountain regions. However, of greater concern, for many people living in coastal areas, the warming of the oceans will ultimately result in rising sea levels. This development is reinforced by melting ice-sheets and glaciers, resulting in increased runoff from large rivers into oceans, which will increase the water volume and thus contribute to rising sea levels. Rising sea levels, in turn, will dramatically increase flood risk and threaten to submerge some areas entirely. Assuming a temperature change of 2.4 degrees Celsius (best estimate for the period 2090–2099 relative to 1980–1999), the anticipated sea level rise is said to be about 0.20–0.45 meters; however, another scenario which assumes a temperature change of four degrees Celsius entails an even larger rise in sea level by about 0.59 meters (IPCC 2007b). This might still be a rather optimistic picture of the future as recent studies conclude that the IPCC sea level projections are too conservative (Rahmstorf 2007). For example, Pfeffer *et al.* (2008) found that a rise of about 2 meters is conceivable by 2100 under extreme conditions. Sea level rise and human development together are contributing to losses of coastal wetlands and mangroves as well as driving damage from coastal flooding in many areas. The consequences are likely to be increased emigration and resettlements: the Stern Review estimates that up to 200 million people could be permanently displaced as a result of sea level rises, flooding, and drought (Stern 2006).

Observational evidence from all continents and most oceans indicate with a high degree of certainty, that **natural ecosystems** will be affected by temperature increases and regional climatic changes (IPCC 2007b). Terrestrial biological systems will experience earlier spring events, such as leaf-unfolding, bird migration, and egg-laying; and pole-ward and upward shifts in ranges in plant and animal species. Humankind will face a severe loss of biodiversity and potentially entire ecosystems: 20 to 30 percent of plant and animal species are likely to be at increased risk of extinction if increases in global average temperature exceed 1.5 to 2.5 degrees Celsius (IPCC 2007b). The Amazon rainforest, for example, is particularly vulnerable to this. Furthermore, ocean acidification will seriously affect marine ecosystems and could lead to a major decline in fish stocks—in addition to the unsustainable overfishing practices in many regions of the world.

For **agriculture** the consequences of these developments are two-fold. First, the increased runoff and earlier spring peak discharge in many glacier- and snow-fed rivers as well as warming of lakes and rivers in many regions will affect thermal structure and water quality. Second, the pole-ward and upward shifts in ranges in plant species will shift crop productivity and food production. These changes will require new strategies for established agricultural and forestry management in the northern hemisphere. Drier regions of the world such as those in Africa face an even more severe risk of declining crop yields.

With respect to **human systems** the IPCC (2007b) illustrates that the likely consequences range from changes that are "easy to bear" to those that are life-threatening. On the one hand, human activities in the Arctic (e.g., shorter hunting and travel seasons over snow and ice) and in lower-elevation alpine areas (e.g., limitations in winter sports) will be affected. These consequences can be addressed by adequate adaptation strategies which, provided that adaptation is not impossible or too expensive, are rather easy to bear. On the other hand, human health can be affected: for example, by excess heat-related mortality, changes in infectious disease vectors, and earlier onset of and increases in seasonal production of allergenic pollen in northern hemisphere high and mid-latitudes. However, the most severe effects can be expected in developing countries where factors such as increased famine, illness, poverty, mass migration, and cross-border conflicts can result in resource wars and political collapse.

## Climate change skeptics

Undeniably, there are and will always be climate change skeptics who continue to emphasize that climate change is just media hype, self-justification of climate researchers, and a phenomenon that has always been occurring. According to these critics, climate change is a self-created political fiasco. One frequent argument that has been made lies in the observation that temperatures have recently stopped increasing (Carter 2006). A closer look at the rather short time frame of temperatures from 1998 onwards does indeed point to—at a first glance—a very striking phenomenon: global average temperature did not increase. However, careful analyses of the IPCC statistics show that this argument does not hold. In 1998 a very strong El Niño event occurred which resulted in abnormally high temperatures, even higher than the average long-term increasing trend. Comparing this peak with a rather short time period afterwards will naturally result in a distorted picture. Given that 1998 was an outlier year in terms of temperature, it is likely that the following years would be lower. This consideration also neglects any long-term developments that have occurred. When considering temperatures over more than 200 years there appears to be a totally different pattern occurring: a long-term trend towards higher global average temperatures. Short-term variations cannot display a general cessation in climate change.

Another frequent argument used by skeptics is that water vapor is by far more relevant for global warming than other greenhouse gases. Water vapor is, in fact, among the larger sources of naturally occurring greenhouse gases. Without water vapor the temperature of the globe would be comparable to that of the inside of a typical freezer. Water vapor is therefore necessary to the survival of our planet's ecosystems. Compared with other greenhouse gases, water vapor only remains in the atmosphere for a very short time. More notably, only a negligible part is emitted as a result of human activities. Therefore, the IPCC does not include water vapor as a human-induced green-house gas. Critics who argue that water vapor is one of the most important greenhouse gases must also understand that changes to the long-term established natural climate equilibrium (to which the concentration of water vapor contributes) are resulting from human-released greenhouse gases (those the IPCC accounts for). To this end, water vapor becomes of interest again: through increasing tempera-tures, more water evaporates and in turn this has an additional effect on the global climatic system—creating a feedback mechanism that accelerates climate change.

The Forum of the Swiss Academy of Sciences summarized the debate about climate skeptics in a recent Climate Press newsletter (SCNAT 2010). The main conclusion is that the arguments of climate skeptics usually follow one or more of the following seven patterns:

1. Research on climate change is not precise and is uncertain; therefore, we do not really know what will happen

2. Presentation of wrong or misleading information; by refer-ring to scientifically wrong information or by picking on just specific and selected details, skeptics base their arguments on inaccurate or insufficient information

3. Climate change is not man-made; we don't have to worry because we are not the cause of the climate crisis

4. Global warming is actually a good thing; in agriculture, for example, yields will increase

5. There were always climatic changes; we don't have to worry because it is a naturally occurring process

6. Protecting the climate is useless; all efforts are too expen-sive, without effect, and thus not necessary

7. It is all a matter of politically motivated fear-mongering; we don't have to worry because reality is not really that bad.

The examples above illustrate how misinterpretation of scientific results, even when presented in a highly scientific and convincing manner, contributes to public confusion in this debate. Although we can provide plenty of examples in this regard (such as the water vapor discussion), we will not take heed of these efforts and will not elaborate on them any further. Instead, we would like to stress how pertinent it is to look at the methods used when analyzing and manipulating the data and to seek out neglected facts. Afterwards, most counter-arguments stemming from climate skeptics become less convincing or even doubtful. Therefore, we highlight a few key points with respect to carbon trends. First, we look at the anthropogenic origin of carbon accumulation. At the beginning, primitive humans survived on Earth in carbon equilibrium for thousands of years with settled agriculture and population increases as the first sources of the human-induced carbon burden. Initially, these were moderate enough not to cause alarming changes in climate. Once humans harnessed energy and started producing it in large quantities, when human development began occurring at an accelerated pace, dramatic changes in the environment began. Second, the frenetic pace of industrialization and population expansion of the past one hundred years has been at a pace that is unparalleled in history. This development also contributes to the current carbon challenges for the Earth's atmosphere. By considering the Earth as a closed system, it becomes obvious that there are certain limitations in terms of the Earth's carrying capacity. We are not claiming that we have reached this limit yet, but current empirical data summarized in the IPCC reports suggests that we are at serious risk of reaching the Earth's greenhouse gas limits. Any climate change skeptics seem to fully neglect these historical facts.

Finally, it is important to be aware that, within the climate debate, for almost every viewpoint surrounding this issue some sort of academic support can be found. But it is crucial to consider how convincing and notably accurate this support actually is. This does not only hold for contra arguments but also for pro climate change arguments. The debate in late 2009 triggered by emails from a climate scientist who seemed to smother certain scientific evidence on purpose is just one prime example of the latter. Nevertheless, even when encountering results of studies that deny climate change as a fact, or seek to dismiss the ecological and social consequences as not severe, one should not neglect those reports that illustrate already observable changes to the climate system. In other words, many reports—acknowledging climate change or not—try to predict the future and derive recommendations on what might come. Although these studies are subject to a certain level of uncertainty regarding future conditions, they base their arguments on the visible effects of actual climatic change. For example, the Arctic Monitoring and Assessment Programme (AMAP 2009) found that several indicators—which assess ecological effects such as decreasing sea ice or the extent of glaciers—show further and extensive changes at rates faster than previously anticipated. This and similar reports do not intend to predict the future; they report on actual changes of the natural system that are occurring in the present. Therefore, whatever one tends to believe about the future of climate change, these facts cannot be denied, as they are not subject to any kinds of uncertainty in scientific assumptions about future developments. In response to many arguments frequently used by climate change skeptics, 250 scholars published their view on climate change and the integrity of science in a recent letter in the journal *Science*:

> There is always some uncertainty associated with scientific conclusions; science never absolutely proves anything. When someone says that society should wait until scientists are absolutely certain before taking any action, it is the same as saying society should never take action. For a problem as potentially catastrophic as climate change, taking no action poses a dangerous risk for our planet (Sills 2010: 689).

# 6

# Carbonomics and beyond

Climate change is predicted to have severe effects not just in environmental and humanitarian terms, but also in its effects on the economy. According to the economist Sir Nicholas Stern (2006), up to a fifth of global economic wealth could be at risk as a result of climate change impacts. In this chapter we summarize economic approaches discussed in literature that are linked to the carbon crisis. We start by elucidating the different perspectives available in terms of how authors assess future costs of climate change. Next we discuss abatement costs that occur when mitigating climate change effects. Lastly, we consider the input dimension of carbon constraints, by focusing on the extraction costs of resources and the corresponding pricing mechanisms. Based on these insights from economic theory, we conclude that a deeper understanding "beyond carbonomics" is required to illustrate the business case for the strategic management of the global carbon crisis.

# The costs of climate change

In the economic literature there exist different views about how future costs associated with climate change should be estimated. One important aspect of this debate is the underlying pricing methods that are used to generate monetary values of climate change-induced damages. In general, at least three methods can be applied. The first method describes the costs of external effects which have a negative side effect on a third party (cf. Baumol 1972). Following this method, costs occur as the originator does not bear the costs associated with the negative side effects. In the context of climate change this implies that companies and individuals who emit greenhouse gases are not made responsible for the long-term damage they cause. In other words, it is assumed that the external costs of a changing climate are not internalized. When assessing the costs of climate change applying this approach, the total amount of damages is estimated that society has to bear. The second method refers to the hedonic pricing method, which estimates changes in economic value resulting from changes in environmental quality (cf. Rosen 1974). This method can be explained with reference to housing prices. For example, when people move to nicer places (e.g., with less air pollution), this increases the demand for housing and consequently impacts prices. As such, the environmental quality of better air conditions becomes a price. Transferring this idea to climate change, it can be estimated how much losses in economic value will be ascribed to climatic changes. The third method is the economics of happiness which emphasizes that, beyond a subsistence level of income, the relative income is also an important indicator for individual well-being (cf. Cohen and Vandenbergh 2008). In this sense, important aspects of life beyond the monetary aspects are considered: for example, leisure time and health. In the climate context, estimates consider the decline in happiness due to climate change and the resulting individual constraints and inconveniences.

These different pricing methods inevitability yield mixed results. Furthermore, studies inherently have to deal with uncertainties and rather long time frames (Tol 2003); both require making assumptions, which influence the results of the models. Moreover, the future costs need to be discounted to the present in order to generate a comparable basis for decision making. There exists quite a bit of debate among economists on the appropriate discount rate to apply. Economist Richard Tol emphasizes that the different estimates of costs related to climate change are driven to a large extent by the choice of the discount rate: a lower discount rate implies a higher estimate and vice versa (Tol 2008). Furthermore, the results also change if costs for adaptation measures are included. That is, on top of damage costs stemming from climate change, adaptation costs could also be considered, which occur from efforts seeking to prevent further damages. In summary, we conclude that there is no consensus at present in the economist's world of what the future costs of climate change are—there is no "true" value for the social costs of climate change. In the following we briefly summarize the results of one very prominent study, the Stern Review. The methods and results of this review are not without critics; for example, in 2006 and 2007 there was an ongoing debate in the journal *World Economics* led by advocates and opponents of the Stern report's positions. In light of our comments above, we do not want to engage in a detailed discussion on this matter; instead we use the report as one prominent example to illustrate the basic procedure of such economic analyses.

The Stern Review on *The Economics of Climate Change* (Stern 2006) was published in October 2006. The report consists of an integrated assessment model that incorporates both climate models and economic models. The two key questions are: (1) what is the welfare reduction due to climate change compared with no climate change; and (2) what are the costs of strategies to reduce carbon dioxide emissions? The underlying basic idea behind these two questions stems from economic equilibrium thinking. In economic theory, the optimal cost of a climate change solution would seek to achieve a greenhouse gas concentration level where the marginal abatement costs (see below) equal the marginal benefits from the damages avoided. Responding to the first question, the average reduction of world GDP per year due to climate change could be about 5–20 percent when assuming business-as-usual paths for emissions up to 2200. However, the answer to the second question reveals that it is much more economically rational to act before then: the review estimates the annual costs of stabilization at 500–550 ppm carbon dioxide equivalents—which is usually referred to as the necessary boundary to keep the global average temperature increase below two degrees Celsius—to be around 1 percent of world GDP by 2050. As such, the simple but very important conclusion of the report is that "the benefits of strong, early action considerably outweigh the costs" (Stern 2006: II).

## Abatement cost curve

Abatement costs are those costs associated with measures seeking to prevent the negative impacts. When analyzing these costs of curbing greenhouse gases, it is important to consider the individual technological solutions. Each technology uses different substitutes for carbon-based materials or seeks to optimize the carbon efficiency in existing systems. As such, each technology is accompanied by specific costs for reducing one ton of greenhouse gases. These are called abatement costs. When considering all existing technologies, the result is the abatement cost curve. The consulting firm McKinsey has estimated such a curve on the global level as shown in Figure 7.

The curve illustrates an estimate of the maximum potential of technological greenhouse gas abatement options at hand across regions and sectors. The measures considered are below €60 per ton of $CO_2$-equivalents and assume a business-as-usual scenario up to 2030. When interpreting the curve it is important to be aware that this was created from an investor's perspective. This means that the specific costs are considered to be additional costs that one would have to bear if the considered alternative is preferred to the status quo. This comparison can only be made based on certain assumptions. As a consequence, the abatement cost curve is often criticized for neglecting certain risks, costs, and socio-psychological factors. For example, the risks of individual technological solutions are neglected. These are important as investors usually take into consideration both the return of an investment as well as its underlying risks. Furthermore, it does not reflect sunk costs. These are relevant as managers often consider the expenses of already existing investments, some of which

Figure 7 **Global GHG abatement cost curve beyond business-as-usual, 2030**

Source: McKinsey & Company: The impact of the financial crisis on carbon economics—Version 2.1 of the Global Greenhouse Gas Abatement Cost Curve

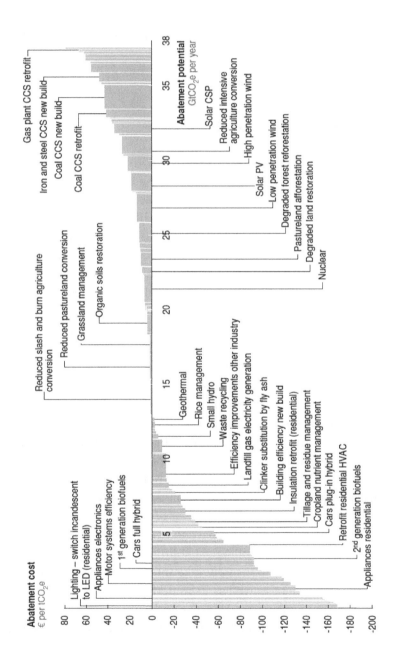

The curve presents an estimate of the maximum potential of all technical GHG abatement measures below €80 per tCO₂e if each lever was pursued aggressively. It is not a forecast of what role different abatement measures and technologies will play.

still need to pay back. Finally, consumer preferences are neglected. Whether private consumers buy a more fuel-efficient and smaller car is always an individual decision based on many psychological factors, such as the need for status. We have to be aware of all the underlying assumptions when working with and interpreting the abatement cost curve.

Nevertheless, Figure 7 illustrates one very interesting element: the availability of technologies that have negative costs. This means that investing in these options will actually generate additional income. As such, it should be very appealing to use these options as they constitute classic win–win solutions. The question that immediately arises is why have these options not yet been realized? The answer to this cannot be fully explained by a purely economic perspective. Instead, also reflecting on the assumptions discussed above, other disciplines are necessary to fully understand the situation. There may be, for instance, several cultural or cognitive biases and habits that can explain why humans and investors will not immediately change their behavior. For example, the rationale behind many day-to-day decisions is based on past experiences. Also, the existence of conflicts of interest between parties must be addressed. One prominent phenomenon to illustrate this point is the so-called landlord–tenant issue. Figure 7 shows that the insulation retrofit of a residence has a negative abatement cost. This means by investing in better insulation, expenditures for heating and cooling of an apartment, for example, can be reduced. This reduction in total is much higher than the initial investment that is required to insulate the apartment. The problem is that the costs of insulating have to be covered by the landlord. The benefits, however, are to the tenants who rent the apartment. The landlord does not have an incentive to invest, as he or she does not receive any revenues from the investment. The tenants also do not have an incentive to incur the costs of this investment, as they do not own the apartment (e.g., they might move out shortly and would risk incurring a sunk cost). Therefore, conducting a cost–benefit analysis does not always yield obvious answers and prompt immediate action. Further agreements between individual actors and parties need to be made. In terms of the landlord–tenant issue, for example, there should be a mutual benefit-sharing agreement.

On the upper end of the abatement cost curve rest several options that are associated with positive costs. This means that by using these options, additional costs will be incurred compared with the status quo. Applying cost–benefit analyses in this context is helpful for comparing the current costs that occur for the required mitigation investment with the future benefits associated with not having to bear the costs of damages. It is important to bear in mind that this is a macro-economic perspective. In a micro perspective, individual companies would need to assess their specific level of abatement costs in relation to the costs of potential greenhouse gas emission regulations. On the macro level, however, the question is whether investing in mitigation options is more profitable than future adaptation expenses. Stern's (2006) answer to this has been discussed already: without any mitigation efforts the damage costs in 2200 could be between 5 and 20 percent of the global gross domestic product. If global emissions were cut in half then damage costs would be 1 percent of the global gross domestic product.

Why is climate change mitigation then not one of the most urgent matters on current policy agendas? The answer to this question is multilayered and discussed more in detail in Chapter 9. However, one reason may be the scope of cost–benefit analyses. The costs of reducing the amount of emissions to a certain level can be determined for a country or region based on the illustrated abatement cost curve. Determining the benefits, however, is more difficult. On the one hand, the benefits are not immediate. Damages that may occur in a time frame up to 2200 are less appealing for policy makers living in a situation of rather short-term election periods. As such, it is usually difficult to find adequate arguments for large-scale mitigation investments. On the other hand, for politicians, national boundaries are usually considered in macro-economic cost–benefit analyses. As such, realized benefits in foreign countries are not factored in. For many industrialized countries this means that a lot of the actual benefits of curbing emissions are not taken into account in national cost–benefit analyses. Even in a global cost–benefit analysis assessing the benefits for a country's income (GDP), a similar issue emerges. In this case, developing nations do not get much weighting. They have relatively low national incomes (compared with industrialized countries). The realized benefits measured as changes in economic value are also rather low. An alternative would be to use different methods to generate monetary values—for example, the previously discussed happiness measure—but these are usually difficult to operationalize. Consequently, the countries that will be most affected by climate change are not factored in an adequate manner. This paradoxical situation is in fact the outcome of the purely economic approach that is commonly used.

## Resource extraction costs and related path dependencies

In Chapter 4, we argued that carbon scarcity would become real for the business environment once markets have started to increase prices. Economists have developed arguments on how and when scarcity should be reflected in markets. In a theoretical discussion about optimal extraction of resources, economist Harold Hotelling (1931) maintained that different resources are used in the order of their specific extraction costs, which can vary depending on geographical accessibility, related transportation costs, or geological differences. The marginal cost of resource extraction and the opportunity cost of a unit of resource in the ground determine the price. As extraction proceeds, the opportunity cost of a unit of the resource should also rise (Ruth 2006). As a result, under the assumption of constant or increasing demand, the price should be negatively correlated to the size of the stock.

What is reality telling us? Probably the most famous debate in this regard goes back to the bet between the economist Julian Simon and ecologist Paul Ehrlich (we referred to the Ehrlich and Holdren formula in Chapter 1). The two professors bet $1,000 on the price development of a basket consisting of five metals (Tierney 1990). The bet was quite easy: Ehrlich proposed an increase in prices while Simon predicted a decline in prices over a ten-year time frame. The result was devastating: despite declining physical resources, the inflation-adjusted price level in 1990 was below the starting point in 1980.

Scientific studies also show support for this empirical experiment. For example, Scott and Pearse (1992) argue that resource prices have not provided significant evidence for scarcity. In contrast, the output of primary resource materials has been growing while their relative prices have declined, mainly through technological improvements. In this context, Reynolds (1999) suggests that exploration costs constitute an adequate measure for scarcity. He assumes that the explorer never entirely knows the size of the resource base. Exploration costs decrease when the explorer gains new information about new reserves as discovery proceeds. As an effect, the true scarcity will not be revealed until the resource is close to exhaustion. This could result in a sudden and sharp increase in resource prices, even after decades of declining prices. Furthermore, path-dependencies are one possible explanation for inefficiencies on resource markets. One reason for path-dependencies could be sunk costs associated with differences in the market value for assets (Antonelli 1997). This circumstance can lead to reduced commitment to the development of large technological innovations and thus delay the substitution of carbon-based inputs with renewable resources.

But are these observations and insights good news? Unfortunately not. Instead of revealing obvious long-term trends, resource markets seem to disguise reality. Looking at the current price for crude oil, it seems that some kind of path-dependency has become a reality. Despite an all-time peak in 2008, prices remained fairly moderate. Although these prices may reflect expectations that crude oil and other fossil fuels are not going to become scarce in the near future, we conclude that current actors' behaviors on markets appear to be biased, at least in the short term. The previously mentioned non-rational facts such as herd behavior determine expectations and behavior on markets and cannot be fully explained by economist approaches. However, we argue that, once natural scarcity has been acknowledged as an emerging issue in the long term, this will prompt markets to incorporate higher risk premiums and will result in an adjustment of prices.

# Beyond pure economic approaches

Having provided short reviews of various economist views of carbon in- and output dimensions, we would like to summarize our findings and point out that there are—as discussed in other contexts (Nelson 1991)—limitations to taking purely economic approaches to the carbon crisis and climate change. With regard to the output dimension we discussed that there is a certain arbitrariness when assessing damage costs owing to the different discount rates used and that there are limitations to cost–benefit analyses. Regarding the input dimension, current actors' behaviors on markets appear to be biased and there is the possibility of certain sudden market disruptions caused by scarcity. Given these factors we demonstrate that there are plenty of other factors—beyond "carbonomics" as discussed above—that are important to fully understand the causes and effects of the global carbon crisis. There are many interdependent and simultaneously occurring causes of carbon accumulation and many different effects within the social, institutional, and natural environments. A dynamic model of the potential causes of the crisis and resulting effects on society and business would at a minimum include the human, organizational, technological, regulatory, infrastructure, and preparedness (HOT+RIP) elements.

## Human elements

It is vital that we overcome biased behaviors on resource markets and move forward in the climate debate despite the limitations of current methods in estimating future developments and costs. Instead we have to acknowledge the inevitable changes and potential solutions that the world is facing. The human population has continued to increase for the past three centuries, and will continue to grow by nearly 50 percent to about nine billion in the middle of the 21st century. The world average per capita consumption is increasing, which is in line with growing aspirations of poorer nations to reach the levels of developed countries. As discussed in the first part of the book, the carbon loading of the environment is a function of population, consumption, and technology. As long as the two technology-related factors, decoupling and decarbonization, cannot even out the increase in carbon loading, the increase in both population and consumption will contribute to further greenhouse gas emission growth and accelerated fossil fuel depletion. In such a case, a radical mind-shift towards low-carbon consumption patterns is necessary. We discussed earlier that, through a sufficiency strategy, individuals could contribute to significant carbon reductions by changing their lifestyles.

## Organizational elements

Industrialization has occurred under conditions in which organizations were allowed to externalize pollution and other negative environmental impacts, climate change probably being the most prominent example. In theory the state was supposed to take care of these externalities by forcing the polluters to internalize the external effects. However, with states perennially running budget deficits and international competition for business-friendly environments, it is not of prime interest to devote resources to address the externalities. Furthermore, a related organizational cause of the present carbon crisis is that corporations and their investors are embedded in short-term reward and profit maximization systems. Managers work to deliver economic performance over the next quarter or year, often ignoring the long-term consequences of their actions, notably regarding the natural environment. As such, the majority of organizations today do not manage costs over ecological life cycles and thus they remain in their carbon-locked-in production paths.

## Technological elements

We positioned the decoupling of economic growth from the use of energy and decarbonization of the energy mix as the key technological challenges ahead. However, in the past there has been a variety of technological shortcomings that have contributed to an emerging carbon crisis. Only over the past thirty years have science and technology of climate change developed enough for us to gauge the damages. Poor understanding of the long-term ecological consequences of technologies has led to highly carbon-intense production processes. In the current situation, the large carbon footprint of aviation technologies and industrial agriculture is further contributing to the emergence of the carbon crisis. Yet the renewable energy fraction of total energy consumption remains limited: 12 percent from established renewable energy sources, such as hydropower and biofuels, and only 0.5 percent from newer technologies relying on wind, solar, wave, and geothermal energy (UN 2007). Unless there is no breakthrough in thinking towards an accelerated diffusion and implementation of existing low-carbon technologies, the necessary decoupling and decarbonization will not be achieved. The important point being made here is: the required technological change does not have to rely on technology breakthroughs; it can be achieved with already existing technologies (ECF 2010).

## Regulatory elements

Carbon dioxide accumulation in the atmosphere could be prevented by regulating the inputs, throughputs, and outputs of the discussed input/output model. Regulating throughputs would need to focus on production technologies. The issue, however, is that regulation of inadequate technologies is usually post hoc. Only after a technology is proven to cause harm do governments seek to regulate it. Afterwards, regulations are implemented partially and often have loopholes. Regarding inputs and outputs the global context is a significant cause of the carbon crisis. As organizations have the ability to shift pollution burdens across national boundaries, they seek to avoid stringent regulations and move highly polluting production facilities to less regulated environments. For example, aluminum production is much more profitable in countries such as China or India compared with EU countries because of the high electricity costs, part of which can be ascribed to the European Union's Emissions Trading Scheme. There are only a few international governance mechanisms to regulate technology harm across the globe: for example, the elimination of CFCs by the Montreal Protocol. For climate change, however, Copenhagen and Cancun demonstrated that it is very difficult to reach an international climate treaty and establish global climate governance structures. One main reason for this lies in the self-interests of some powerful governments and states. Susan George (2010) critically reflects on this phenomenon in her book *Whose Crisis,*

*Whose Future?* by referring to power and interests of what she calls the "transnational neoliberal elite." In summary, regulatory short-comings are responsible for the current lack of national and international climate policy enforcement mechanisms. The sources of these political shortcomings and strategic options at hand are discussed in more detail in Chapter 9.

## Infrastructure elements

Much of the carbon dioxide released into the Earth's atmosphere can be related to the established infrastructure settings. There is little commensurate development of the policy infrastructure, physical infrastructure, and technologies needed to mitigate these increases. Many of these systems are highly carbon- and path-dependent. For example, the entire transportation system relies mainly on fossil fuels. To date, efforts in the direction of electro-mobility have been honorable. But as long as the electricity mix is not decarbonized such efforts will not contribute to significant greenhouse gas reductions. This requires life-cycle-wide considerations of reduction potentials. Likewise for the building sector, significant energy efficiency improvements are needed as buildings today account for 40 percent of the world's energy use (WBCSD 2009). These require the design of new efficiency programs targeting not-yet-realized carbon improvements in private housing and commercial buildings (ECF 2010). For example, the World Business Council for Sustainable Development (WBCSD 2009) has calculated that at energy prices proportionate to oil at $60 per barrel, investments in increasing building energy efficiency can reduce the energy use and corresponding carbon dioxide emissions by about 40 percent assuming a five-year discounted payback for the owners.

## Preparedness elements

The widespread failure of communities to prepare for emerging carbon constraints is another important cause of the carbon crisis. Communities most at risk are simply ignorant of the scale and urgency of climate-change-causing mechanisms. Many argue that knowledge about climate change is complicated, with scientific uncertainty, and is politically contentious. Another contributing factor is the lack of values of ecological stewardship. In response, many communities are unprepared and lack political will to change their historical behaviors. Only a few communities have started to move towards a low-carbon future. For instance, New York's Mayor Michael Bloomberg announced the objective to reduce the city's carbon dioxide emissions by 30 percent by 2030 compared with 2005.[1] London's Mayor Boris Johnson pursues an even more ambitious objective. He intends to reduce emissions by about 60 percent by 2025 taking 1990 as baseline.[2] However, beyond these and a few other examples, there is little community-wide concern for preserving nature beyond its immediate utilitarian value. Nature is mostly treated as a resource or an asset to be exploited. This orientation, coupled with short-term capitalistic interests, results in the rapacious exploitation of fossil fuels and emission of carbon dioxide to the atmosphere. However, it is important that communities as well as businesses worldwide acknowledge the need to address the carbon crisis—this is of no less capitalistic interest, at least in the long term.

1  www.nyc.gov/html/om/pdf/2009/pr465-09_plan.pdf (accessed February 18, 2011)
2  www.tfl.gov.uk/assets/downloads/corporate/Item13-TfL-Climate-Change-Response.pdf (accessed February 18, 2011).

# 7

# The intra- vs. inter-generational equity dimension

Resolving the carbon crisis and creating a world that is sustainable for more than nine billion people will require an overall reduction in total consumption and production—at least under current carbon-dependent production systems and without any widespread radical low-carbon innovations. This raises the pivotal issue of equity. Who should reduce, by how much, and when? These questions bear an actor and a time component. The actor component refers to the intra-generational equity dimensions while the time component refers to the inter-generational equity dimension.

## The global carbon crisis in our generation

With respect to the intra-generational equity dimension, two questions raised are: who is responsible for the emerging carbon crisis and who will suffer the most? The answer to the former can be found just by looking at the globe during the night. This unequivocally shows who is consuming the largest amount of energy: the developed countries shine bright, whereas the developing countries remain dark. This energy consumption correlates with the level of per capita carbon footprint. Figure 8 illustrates this bipolar relationship between developing and developed countries illustrating the carbon dioxide emissions per capita in 2006. With respect to the question who will suffer the most, investigations suggest that developed nations will be the least negatively affected by climate change given their annual GDP, and some developed nations may even be affected in a positive way (e.g., Dell *et al.* 2008). However, the same studies usually reveal that the majority of countries and people in the developing world will face severe negative effects. Therefore, the regions that contribute the greatest to climate change (industrialized countries) are not the regions that will suffer the most from its effects. The major impacts will first fall on developing countries, such as Africa, which will have to cope with less water availability and reduced agricultural yields (UNDP 2007). Many small islands might even vanish because of rising sea levels. Poor nations, such as Bangladesh, which have large populations in low-lying areas, are also likely to experience much larger flood damages. The connection between regional cause and effects is very poorly understood.

This intra-generational regional equity issue has at least three dimensions. One involves the ethics of differential impacts. How can we ethically justify the inequity in development across the globe, particularly when some in the industrialized world are living highly carbon-intensive lifestyles while two-thirds of the world population lives in poverty? Forty percent of the world's population accounts for five percent of world income, while the richest 20 percent accounts for three-quarters of world income (UNDP 2007). And a recent World Bank report found that extreme poverty is even more pervasive than previously expected (Chen and Ravallion 2008). It is estimated that one-quarter of the population of the developing world lived below $1.25 a day in 2005. Although the poverty rate in East Asia fell from almost 80 percent to under 20 percent between the 1980s and 2005, it stagnated at around 50 percent in sub-Saharan Africa. The poorest 10 percent of the world account for 1.5 percent of the global private

## Figure 8  Carbon footprint of selected nations 2006 (carbon dioxide emissions per capita)

Source: World Development Indicators, data.worldbank.org/indicator (accessed February 27, 2011)

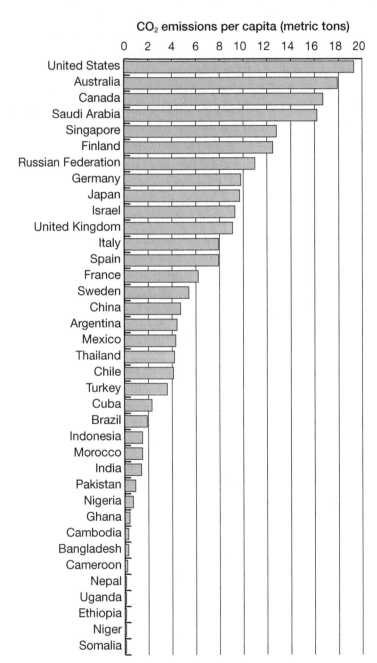

consumption, while the richest 10 percent account for about 60 percent.[1] There is no ethical basis to stop economic development from occurring in developing nations. The issue is that many of these developing nations do not have clean technologies to fuel growth because of the stage of economic development which most of these nations are in. However, to ask all nations to equally share the burdens of cutting back development would sound hypocritical. The only morally acceptable position may be for developed nations to allow developing nations to at least reach a certain level of development where they can feed their populations.

The second dimension of regional equity is the political feasibility of enforcing differential development. Currently, international climate and energy governance mechanisms remain weak. Economic incentives, sanctions, and social pressures are not enough to ensure change on a large scale. Under such circumstances it is not going to be politically feasible to stop developing nations (notably China and India) from emulating the carbon-intensive lifestyle of the West. Both of these countries already have large middle-class populations (over 300 million each), who are mimicking the patterns of consumption that are prevalent in developed countries.

The third dimension of regional equity is the "security" aspects of environmental degradation. Climate change impacts have immense security implications for different countries (UNDP 2007). We discussed earlier that some developed nations may be affected in a positive way while the majority of countries and people in the developing world will face severe negative effects. As climate changes progressively take effect, some parts of the Earth will be unable to sustain life as they currently do, while other areas will find new natural resources and productivity. Presumably, this will fuel mass population migrations that will be largely destabilizing if not managed properly.

Since ecological problems cross national boundaries we need to think of systemic solutions. Recently, the State of Colorado voted to pay for use of clean coal technology in China. Reason being, the dirty coal used in China was resulting in smoke being mixed in with

1  www.globalissues.org/article/26/poverty-facts-and-stats (accessed February 27, 2011).

clouds, traveling across the world and raining down on Colorado ski slopes. This was melting the snow earlier than normal, thereby shortening the ski season, causing billions of dollars of lost revenue each year (Colorado's major industry is skiing). By helping China clean up their coal, Colorado could recoup their revenues. This interconnectivity of the natural ecosystem is the central justification for systemic global solutions.

Furthermore, beyond these regional considerations of intra-generational equity is the equity issue between poorer and richer individuals, independent of whether they live in the developed or the developing world. Carbon constraints will be most visible through price increases. These price increases primarily pertain to oil, gas, and electricity. As such, the everyday use of energy and transportation will become much more expensive. With energy and transportation as necessary components for most production processes, the prices of all other commodities will also increase. This will cause poorer individuals to experience a significant reduction in their purchasing capacity, with most of these individuals coming from developing countries.

## The global carbon crisis between generations

The Global Footprint Network estimates that the carbon footprint makes up 50 percent of humanity's overall ecological footprint (see Fig. 9) and, notably, is the most rapidly growing and uncertain component. The network concludes that reducing humanity's carbon footprint is the most essential step towards living within the means of our planet.

While the above discussion on intra-generational equity is concerned with equity between people of the same generation, inter-generational equity is about equity between present and future generations. Sustainable development is about meeting the needs of the current generation without jeopardizing the ability of future generations to meet their needs. An example is the forest-dwelling

Figure 9  **Humanity's ecological footprint**

Source: Global Footprint Network 2011

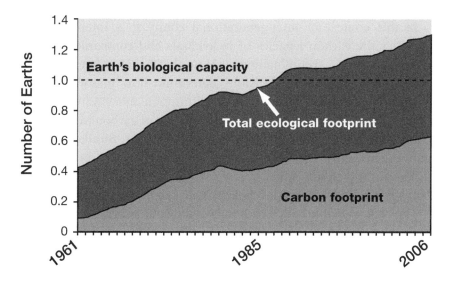

The term "carbon footprint" is often used as shorthand for the amount of carbon (usually in tonnes) that is emitted by an activity or organization. The carbon component of the ecological footprint takes a slightly different approach. Here the amount of carbon dioxide is translated into the amount of productive land and sea area required to sequester carbon dioxide emissions.

people in Papua New Guinea who for generations have lived in a certain part of the land using the forest. Now, however, the trees are being sold for palm oil to make money. If this is done at an unsustainable rate there will be no resources left for their children or grandchildren in the future. This unsustainable use of resources leads to inter-generational inequity. Specifically focusing on climate change, the *Human Development Report 2007/2008* (UNDP 2007: 2) highlights the consequences if no action is taken:

> During the 20th Century failures of political leadership led to two world wars. Millions of people paid a high price for what were avoidable catastrophes. Dangerous climate change is the avoidable catastrophe of the 21st Century and beyond. Future generations will pass a harsh judgment on a generation that looked at the evidence on climate change, understood the consequences and then continued

> on a path that consigned millions of the world's most vul-
> nerable people to poverty and exposed future generations
> to the risk of ecological disaster.

In this context of inter-generational equity it is interesting to consider the carbon legacies of individuals and companies. These legacies refer to carbon loadings that are left behind after we pass. Individual reproductive decisions determine how many children we leave behind. Our lifestyle and consumption choices are handed down to these future generations and patterns of carbon loading are continued through behaviors learned from parents. Similarly, companies leave carbon legacies through their product and production decisions, and technological choices. We lack good measures of carbon legacies and need to develop new ways of thinking about them.

The unsustainable use of carbon-based resources and materials of the current generation results in two main consequences for future generations. First, the overconsumption of fossil fuels will result in carbon scarcity. As discussed before, the natural limitations imposed by our environment impact future generations and their ability to cope with depleting fossil fuel reserves. This entails some severe consequences with respect to future energy production, transportation, and business models, notably as no region—neither developed nor developing—is currently decarbonizing its energy supply (Raupach *et al.* 2007). The vision of a decarbonized society needs to be based on different structures and requires different technologies to maintain a certain level of wealth for future generations.

Second, it is important to recognize that there is a time lag between greenhouse gas emissions and their warming effects in the atmosphere. The temperature increases that are currently being experienced are due to the accelerated emission levels over the last 200 years. The so-called oceanic thermal inertia causes a lag or damping effect, which means that the climate system will continue to change for many decades (centuries for sea level) even in the absence of any future changes in the atmospheric composition (Wigley 2005). Furthermore, it is estimated that the climatic change that takes place is largely irreversible for roughly 1,000 years after carbon dioxide emissions stop (Solomon *et al.* 2009). Therefore, the burden of current emissions will be carried by future generations. Many reports such as those from the IPCC try to predict the likely consequences for future generations. In Chapter 5 we already discussed the likely consequences for weather patterns, the global water system, natural ecosystems, agriculture, and human systems. Based on this, we will now provide a summary of some of the major consequences that future generations will face on a warmer planet.

Water availability will decrease in many areas, and this will be particularly severe in arid and semi-arid developing regions. This will cause further increases in drought, impacting agriculture, and creating famine. Climate change is also an added risk in regions that are already experiencing desertification. All this is likely to lead to resource conflict, as illustrated by a recent event that took place in Bhopal, India. Three members of a family were murdered after having filled containers with water from a pipe that was previously empty for days. The neighbors accused them of stealing (Chamberlain 2009). Although an isolated event, such occurrences are set to become more widespread and on a larger scale in the future as water and other natural resources dwindle.

An increase in storms, cyclones, and sea level will destroy infrastructure such as ports, sewer systems, and energy generators, which are important for economic development. These events will also increase the risk of disease and destroy homes. For example, a sea level rise of 1 meter could destroy up to 46 million homes in Bangladesh and Egypt (Reynolds 2002). It is the poor, low-lying coastal regions or small island states (Asia, the Maldives) which are largely under the threat from rising sea levels, flooding, and severe storms. These changes have the potential to cause extensive loss of life from drowning and diseases (malaria, cholera, yellow fever, and dysentery), destroy crops or make land unviable for agricultural use through salinization, further increasing the risk of famine.

Agriculture, tropical forests, and fish probably face the greatest threats from the carbon crisis. Agriculture, for example, is likely to be negatively affected by the crisis as a result of changes in temperature, precipitation, soil moisture, soil fertility, length of the growing season, and severity of storms (McGuigan *et al.* 2002). Fisheries are also likely to become more and more affected. This is particularly worrying because fish is an important source of protein for many developing countries and thus the predicted changes in fish stocks due to climate change could have devastating consequences, both in terms of world hunger and livelihoods. It is estimated that in the current generation over 200 million people worldwide are economically dependent on fisheries (McGuigan *et al*. 2002). In future generations these people will have to find adequate alternatives.

Currently, poorer nations rely mostly on natural resources for their livelihoods, according to the initial findings of The Economics of Ecosystems and Biodiversity (TEEB) Review 2008. As such these nations will struggle the most in dealing with any health crises, food and water shortages, environmental disasters, and other related crises caused by climate change. One consequence of this is that environmental refugees are likely to become a growing global issue. The Global Humanitarian Forum has estimated that up to 75 million people are likely to be displaced in the next 25 years as a consequence of climate change-related events, such as rising sea levels and flooding, desertification, and resource conflicts (Vidal 2009). This inevitable future can already be seen in areas such as Bangladesh and Zambia. The above examples show that, in many areas, the actions of the current generation contribute to conditions that will have severe effects on future generations.

## Conclusion: the global carbon crisis from an equity perspective

Current emissions will affect both equity dimensions: on the one hand, future generations will have to cope with the negative consequences of a warmer planet; on the other hand, poorer nations will be most negatively affected. If humankind does not want to be in total breach of any equity claims, urgent action is needed now, more than ever. It is important to accelerate efforts to restructure established carbon-intensive production and consumption patterns in industrialized countries; this shift will not take place overnight since massive investments in technology and infrastructure are required. In doing so, the industrialized world can take a leading role by preventing developing countries from further imitating the carbon-intensive industrial revolution of the developed world.

In order to accelerate the pace towards a global low-carbon society, we would like to refer to Edith Brown Weiss (1989) who offers a remarkable approach when searching for ways to address equity questions. Her approach may serve as a kind of a role model for our strategic thinking. Her initial idea focuses on inter-generational aspects; intra-generational equity aspects can, however, easily be integrated in the global carbon crisis context. She differentiates between three general equity principles:

## Conservation of options

> Each generation should be required to conserve the diversity of the natural and cultural resource base, so that it does not unduly restrict the options available to future generations in solving their problems and satisfying their own values, and should be entitled to diversity comparable to that of previous generations (Weiss 1989: 38).

As such, the quintessence of the principle of conservation of options is in the carbon crisis context: all members of the current generation as well as future generations should be able to have the same options based on utilizing fossil fuels and emitting greenhouse gases.

## Conservation of quality

> Each generation should be required to maintain the quality of the planet so that it is passed on in no worse condition than the present generation received it, and should be entitled to a quality of the planet comparable to the one enjoyed by previous generations (Weiss 1989: 38).

Following this, the quintessence of the principle of conservation of quality is in the carbon crisis context: all members of the current generation as well as future generations should experience a natural environment with the same quality. This entails that there is neither ecological damage caused by climate change nor severe disruption of nature as was the case with the recent BP oil spill in the Gulf of Mexico.

## Conservation of access

> Each generation should provide its members with equitable rights of access to the legacy from past generations and should conserve this access for future generations (Weiss 1989: 38).

Again in the carbon crisis context, the quintessence of the principle of conservation of access is: all members of the current generation as well as future generations should be able to have access to carbon-based resources. This entails that all people around the world are equally able to use fossil fuels and there will be no depletion of fossil fuels before adequate substitutes are available.

The key question then is: How to initiate the required urgent action? In this second part of the book we discussed that there will always be critics present in the debate on climate change and the availability of fossil fuels—probably well funded by certain interest groups. Despite uncertainties about the exact pattern of future temperature change resulting from climate change and the actual time component in the disposition of fossil fuels due to unsustainable carbon utilization patterns, the predicted consequences as discussed above illustrate that it is prudent to act now and prevent a global carbon crisis from becoming a reality (precautionary principle). It is therefore in the best interests of current and future generations that we overcome existing barriers and obstacles. This requires three time-related changes: acknowledging that the implementation of climate-safe policies cannot wait many more years; recognizing a need for an immediate and radical shift in strategic management thinking regarding low-carbon business strategies; and understanding that technologies required are long-term investments. In light of the amplification of physical effects via feedback mechanisms (see Chapter 5), policy makers, businesses, and consumers must recognize the limited time available to begin making necessary changes.

While the main responsibility of reinforcing action and addressing the three equity principles on a global scale lies with governments and international organizations, there are also implications for companies and their strategy formulation. Throughout the book we have highlighted that, for businesses, carbon constraints emerge in the in- and output dimension. Can companies address constraints in both dimensions simultaneously? How can the three equity principles be followed and implemented in daily business life? What is the role of policy and inter-firm collaboration in this respect? The third and last part of our book will provide some answers in this regard.

# Part III
# Strategic options for a low-carbon economy

# 8

# Lessons from the financial crisis

Achim Steiner, the Executive Director of the United Nations Environment Programme (UNEP), recently made a pivotal statement that serves as the motivation for this chapter: "In a time when climate change is a really major challenge for us, to simply deal with the financial crisis and not use that as an opportunity to accelerate our response to global warming would be a tragedy." As such, we should not see the financial crisis as a problem that must be solved as quickly and as simply as possible and, instead, view it as an opportunity to overhaul the economic system and learn from past mistakes—it holds important lessons for the emerging carbon crisis. With this chapter, we compare both crises and draw on parallels and differences, which will help us to better understand paths to preventing a global carbon crisis.

## Origins of the global financial crisis

The global financial crisis that originated in the subprime mortgage market in the US in 2008 has spread to all major financial markets around the world. The causes of the financial crisis are many. One main cause was that the global financial system became too complex, too interconnected and too obscure even for many specialists to assess and manage risks. It was also governed by many rules and regulations, national and international standards, specific financial product/service features, and technological systems that contributed to the complexity and the unmanageability of the risks. It was impossible for auditors and overseers such as federal agencies, state agencies, self-regulatory organizations, and international coordination bodies to clearly know what exactly went on within financial companies and how they constructed new investment products. For example, as was seen in the case of Bernie Madoff, despite all the financial market oversight, he was still able to operate a $65 billion Ponzi scheme, which turned out to be a financial disaster.

The International Monetary Fund estimated that at the beginning of 2009 the number of bad loans globally amounted to around $2 trillion (IMF 2009), much of which originated in the subprime mortgage lending in the US. These represented loans for which mortgage companies and banks lent to unqualified buyers, who had insufficient or no equity. Given that buyers were not putting up any money, when asset prices deteriorated, their response was to walk away from the loans and give up the asset. The lenders, however, also kept no stake in the asset because they sold the risky loans to investment banks or mortgage companies (Fannie Mae or Freddie Mac), who in turn securitized the loans (mortgage-backed securities) and sold them to investors (banks, pension funds, etc.). At the end of the day everyone passed the risk along to the next level in a chain without even knowing what the underlying risks were. This phenomenon is known as the US real estate bubble. The bursting of the bubble caused a significant shock for the entire financial system; many banks were left with enormous levels of bad debt and some banks even became insolvent. As an effect, banks became reluctant to do business with one another and unwilling to lend, which shut down the credit flow considerably and impacted the global economy as a whole.

Governments and corporate managers ignored the warning signals of an impending crisis. Risk metrics used by Wall Street to gauge leverage were telling management that their risk profile was increasing to dangerous levels. Historically, ten-to-one leverage was considered high. At the beginning of the financial crisis the leverage of major investment and securities firms had reached thirty to one and some were operating at fifty-to-one leverage. Auditors, analysts, ratings companies, government agencies, and congressional counterparts all ignored these high leverage levels, letting the financial bubble build up to unsustainable levels. A classic case showing that when everyone is making money no one wants to blow the whistle.

This global financial crisis became a reality; economic turmoil resulted and it continues to shape a changing business environment. We are now faced with dire short-term effects and left to manage the long-term consequences (see Table 6). In the current situation, we can look back into the past in order to make better decisions for the future. What can we learn from the financial crisis so as to prevent a potential global carbon crisis from becoming a reality and hitting global society in a similar—or even worse—in a devastating manner? In order to answer this question, we first compare the short- and long-term effects of the financial crisis with the likely effects of a global carbon crisis. We then elaborate on the parallels and differences of both crises. As the central conclusion of these comparisons

Table 6 **Short- and long-term effects of the financial and carbon crisis**

|  | **Changing business environment** | |
|---|---|---|
|  | **Short- and mid-term** | **Long-term** |
| **Financial crisis** | • Lending/equity gap <br> • Asset price collapse <br> • Bankruptcy/ nationalization of banks | • Reduced economic growth <br> • Redistribution of wealth <br> • Restructuring of governance structures in the banking sector |
| **Carbon crisis** | • Emerging carbon constraints <br> • Volatile energy markets <br> • Increased migration | • Reduced economic growth <br> • Reorientation for maintaining energy security <br> • Resource and territorial conflicts |

we derive lessons from the financial crisis, which may help prevent a global carbon crisis.

## Short- and mid-term effects

The financial crisis brought about a lending/equity gap and an ensuing asset price collapse, which in turn resulted in governments bailing out the banking sector and the nationalization of banks. The short-term effort to infuse capital into banks was an early response to the financial crisis. However, most banks were already operating with a siege mentality and were afraid to lend money to anyone, notably companies that urgently needed debt capital. This credit freeze expanded the crisis from the financial sector to all other sectors of the economy and eventually spread the crisis globally causing an asset price collapse. As businesses slowed down, stock markets lost 30 to 50 percent of value and investors were apprehensive. They started hoarding their money in low-interest Treasury securities, commodities, and gold. Although stock markets have recovered slightly since this asset price collapse, major economies (USA, China, Germany, and Japan) have experienced serious recessions. The United Nations (UN 2010) estimated that global GDP fell by 2.2 percent in 2009, the first time since the World War II. In this situation some banks were not able to continue running their business; the result was bankruptcy or the nationalization of the bank. Premised on continued supportive policy efforts worldwide, a moderate growth is forecast for the mid term (the next couple of years). National governments thus were spending trillions of dollars to stabilize markets and unfreeze credit. In the first year of the crisis the US government had committed $4 trillion, the European Union $2.5 trillion, and China over $1 trillion into market stabilization and economic stimulus measures. They are pumping fresh (i.e., just printed) money into the economy with the hope of mid-term recovery. The vision of recovery unfortunately is restoring the economies to their prior performance levels. This is unfortunate because it misses the opportunity to fundamentally restructure the economy in sustainable directions.

Considering the emergence of a global carbon crisis, the likely—
and partly already real—course in the short and mid term follows a
similar logic: companies and markets will start realizing that fossil
fuel consumption and the emission of greenhouse gases matter from
a financial point of view. Customers will also start considering low-
carbon features as a part of their buying criteria as costs for using
and emitting carbon increase. Financial markets will increasingly
request companies to disclose and manage their carbon liabilities,
and governments will engage in more discussions on new emission
regulations and carbon taxes. These shifts result in emerging carbon
constraints for business, which have to be considered a serious risk
factor for corporate strategy (Busch and Hoffmann 2007). This situation is likely to cause volatility in commodity and energy markets.
The most common and visible example in this regard is the recent
oil price history: after an all-time high in 2008, there was a sharp
decline. Since then, however, prices have been increasing again, but
there are severe fluctuations. This level of volatility in the markets
indicates that there is high uncertainty about future oil availability
and demand resulting in price fluctuations. As volatile oil prices are
already a reality today, other commodities are also likely to follow,
which leads us to the conclusion that the entire energy market has to
be considered a business sector with a high level of uncertainty about
future business conditions. These conditions, in turn, determine the
preferences of people and businesses in terms of where to live, work,
and produce. Energy is and will continue to be the artery for human
life and industrial production. Expensive and uncertain energy
supply will put the entire economic development on a downward
turn: firms face additional costs and risks and postpone necessary
investments; banks become more risk-averse and reduce their lending activities; consumers adjust their consumption patterns; firms'
competitiveness and revenues decrease. The vicious circle is started:
the quality and quantity of energy supply hinder global economic
prosperity and human well-being. Additionally, these developments
will result in increased migration, at least in the mid term. Regions
where such conditions are still superior, where there is still a sufficient, ensured, and reasonably priced energy supply, for example
because of a protected market or huge domestic fossil fuel reserves,

grow in attractiveness and experience a high rate of immigration. In contrast, regions such as Africa with no or limited expensive energy access already face increasing emigration.

## Long-term effects

There is no consensus among economists about when the world economy will fully recover from the recent financial crisis; however, there seems to be uniform opinion that one day it will. Nevertheless, the financial crisis coincides with reduced economic growth in the long term. In the short term, government programs (e.g., cash-for-clunkers) and subsidies (e.g., for industrial companies) have prevented a serious crash of the world economy, as was the case with the Wall Street crash of 1929 and the ensuing Great Depression. However, these programs and subsidies only have a temporary effect. In some cases, these forms of assistance might be able to stimulate innovation processes and perhaps allow individual companies to realize that a serious shift in their business strategy is required in order to maintain long-term competitiveness. In other cases, however, the financial support by governments just delays the effect of the economic downturn for individual firms and industries. The real consequences may even be an accelerated downward effect on individual firms and industries once the financial support stops. Although the economy may recover in major part, this will result in a reduction of GDP.

Along with this primary effect of reduced economic growth in the long run, there is a redistribution of wealth, which will be feasible in three dimensions. First, the reduction in economic growth is most real for working-class people. They have to face higher unemployment rates, reduced purchasing power, and cuts in social welfare systems. People in upper classes certainly also have to cope with similar cutbacks; however, these do not result in such serious reductions of their wealth in their economic and social well-being. Second, the argument above can be extended to the North–South debate, which we discussed in the intra-generational equity context. Emerging markets, particularly those concerned with export quotas, are severely affected by a reduction in global economic activity and the decline in consumer spending as this constitutes a major part of their national income. As such, developing countries are exposed to a relatively higher degree of diminishing wealth. Third, the financial support programs, which are currently being implemented by governments, are usually funded via national debts. These debts enable current generations to maintain a certain level of wealth. However, future generations will have to bear these debts to the detriment of their own wealth. Therefore, there is also a clear redistribution of wealth between the current and future generations caused by the financial crisis.

Certain parts of the banking sector—i.e., the investment bankers that were responsible for developing "innovative" financial products such as mortgage-backed securities—are often held responsible for the financial crisis. However, the origins and causes are multiple and intertwined and cannot be solely attributed to a mere failure of a certain part of the financial system. The individual roles of the decline in mortgage prices, asset–liability mismatch, withdrawals by depositors, previous areas of cheap money (Federal Reserve System), speculative bubbles, and bonus-payment systems in the emergence of the financial crisis shall not be discussed here in detail. Nevertheless, it is important to be aware of the complex underlying cause–effect mechanisms that resulted in the financial crisis. Considering the banking sector as a whole, many people, notably politicians, feel that something went wrong within the system and that rules are needed in order to prevent a similar situation from occurring again. As a consequence, the banking sector faces and will continue to face a restructuring of established governance systems. New and old institutions with new authority will exert their power and control over global and local money flows. Risks will have to be more transparent and the sector will be subject to much more political influence.

Assuming global carbon crisis becomes reality, disruptions in energy supply and consequences of climate change would have severe economic implications. These would stem from adaptation measures on mainly two levels. First, as a result of the carbon crisis there will likely be need for increased and diverted investments for adaptation purposes. This would cause additional costs: for example, in order to protect against or fix damages caused by extreme weather events, which are predicted to occur more often as a consequence of climate change. This in turn would result in fewer investments in other areas. In addition, a general increase in the prices of fossil fuels and certain commodities would reduce economic growth.

Second, a sudden reorientation of the energy system will require an adaptation process that is accompanied by unusually high costs. Low-carbon technologies—which will become a necessity in the long run owing to fossil fuel scarcity and political efforts to mitigate climate change—are still young and are not well diffused. Yet many firms and industries still remain focused on old, carbon-intensive technologies. For example, most of the new electricity generation capacity currently installed in China is coal-based and not renewable. However, implementing new production techniques as well as replacing already existing production facilities with low-carbon technologies such as wind and solar power will take some time. Similarly, gasoline supply systems need to be adjusted in order to pave the way for a new low-carbon transportation system, based on electricity or hydrogen. Therefore, it is important to start investing now in the necessary energy system-wide transformations, to allow smooth and controlled change of the energy system. This adaptation and the required investments have to be part of a long-term and thorough planned strategy. If the carbon crisis became a reality, short-term readjustments and quick-fix solutions would require significantly higher investments and consequently result in suboptimal outcomes, accompanied by negative effects on economic growth.

Continuing on the assumption that the carbon crisis emerges, aspects such as energy supply, energy security, and water availability would be major concerns in the future. A sufficient lack of these conditions would very likely result in resource and territorial conflicts. Both these issues are a problem not only in terms of basic human welfare, but also for industrial processes, agriculture, and economic development as a whole. This can create a very gloomy future of long-lasting social unrest, political instability, and conflict ("water wars," etc.).

# Parallels between both crises

## The *ex ante* knowledge phenomenon

Just as the perils of the US real estate bubble were well known before the bubble burst, so are the phenomena surrounding climate change, carbon, and energy. As has been discussed in this chapter, lending practices in the US real-estate sector and risk appraisals in some parts of the financial sector were unsustainable by any standards. The second part of the book also discussed the notion of how carbon practices are unsustainable at the current rate. Both the financial and the carbon crisis have been documented *ex ante* by experts (financial specialists, environmental scientists) and the media prior to the main collapse. Prior to the global financial crisis, crises in Mexico (1994), the Far East (1997), Russia (1998), and Brazil (1998) demonstrated that the established financing mechanisms and non-transparent risk appraisals can result in financial collapse (Valdez 2000); however, few lessons were learned: the warnings were ignored. In just the same manner, no significant action is being taken regarding the carbon crisis despite clear warning signs (e.g., the melting ice shelf in Antarctica). For both crises it is clear that there is a need to modify the way in which we live on a global scale: by reconstructing financial mechanisms and governance systems, by phasing out fossil fuels and emitting less greenhouse gases. We conclude that the existence of this *ex ante* knowledge is obfuscated, mainly because of information asymmetries. In the financial markets, the initial "product" developers were aware of the high risk of individual loans. But this risk, especially in its aggregated forms, was not visible to the final investor. In the carbon crisis, despite warnings by thousands of serious scientists and ecologists about the devastating consequences of fossil fuel scarcity and climate change, we continue to take the established carbon conditions for granted—and even accelerate the utilization of fossil fuels and emission of greenhouse gases. And the fact that people are not more worried about a carbon crisis and alter their behavior is the result of well-organized and well-funded lobbying and advertising (Levy 2010).

## No decoupling from the economic system

Financial markets and the natural environment are, at first glance, only indirectly linked to the economic system. One could argue that a failure on financial markets primarily affects the financial system and ecological damage primarily affects the natural system. But this is not true per se; neither the financial nor the natural system is decoupled from the economic system. Companies are embedded in the financial and the natural system and as such there is a lagged effect on the entire economic system. Both have a very strong indirect effect on the financial system; in reality there is no decoupling. The various levels of embeddedness entails that the financial and the carbon crisis have far more severe consequences on other systems. However, before the negative effects are tangible, the "decoupled thesis" seems to be more plausible than the "embeddedness thesis"— this holds for both crises. Part of this phenomenon can be attributed to the lack of internalization; in both crises those who cause the externalities are not made responsible for remedying them. With the financial crisis, there has been no internalization of externalities; there was no incentive for more careful speculation. Instead, society at large currently foots the bill for economic failure, while those ostensibly responsible for this failure continue to be subsidized. In terms of the carbon crisis, the externalities caused by greenhouse gas emissions are not internalized either. In regimes where they are regulated the system is still relatively ineffective (see Chapter 9). As there is no global carbon price, the negative consequences of carbon hazards have to be borne by surrounding communities (although the real carbon externalities will become visible only in future).

We therefore conclude that it is important to realize that carbon issues and climate change should not be viewed as just ecological issues. Both are strategically relevant and are not decoupled from the economic system, even as the full negative consequences are not yet apparent. The same was seen in the financial crisis where there was a ripple effect on a global level owing to problems arising from loan issues of US mortgage owners. Taking what was experienced in the financial crisis, one can conjecture how severe the effects of a global carbon crisis might be.

## Global interconnectedness

The financial crisis has illustrated how collective individual actions might cause global problems. However, pushing individuals to change their behavior becomes extremely difficult particularly if they themselves are not greatly affected by the resulting problem. During the '80s and '90s financial shocks were mostly regional (i.e., the Asia crisis, Russian crisis). As a result of the burst of the dot.com bubble in 2001 and the accounting scandals in 2002 there were some severe consequences on financial markets; but markets recovered relatively quickly (Valdez 2007). As such, these crises did not result in the same global consequences as the latest financial crisis. The increasingly globalized and interlinked financial market also means that there are new mechanisms by which financial problems can be transmitted among them. A collapse on Wall Street affects financial institutions throughout the world and has an impact on job losses, poverty, and other social consequences. Initially there were expectations of a financial decoupling between emerging markets and Western economies where the crisis developed. This did not happen, and instead the emerging markets were hit hardest by lack of investment, collapse in trade, and fall in commodity prices. Poor nations suffered most from problems caused by the industrialized world. This global interconnectedness also holds true for the carbon crisis. For example, carbon-intensive industries in the US contribute to rising sea levels in Asia. We conclude that both crises are not limited to national boundaries and therefore there is a need for a greater understanding of the global interconnectedness.

## Limited capacity of policy governance structures

The deregulation of the financial markets resulted in extreme financial risk-taking and speculation. What has been taught to us by the financial crisis is that a minimum of regulations and policies—however well intentioned they may have been—were limited in capacity to enforce safe and stable financial markets. The crisis also has shown that although single actors can reduce their own, individual risk, individualistic behaviors often exacerbate risks for others, which may result in an overall system collapse. The lack of policy enforced governance structures is typical in the carbon and climate context. Individual countries fear the danger of becoming economically disadvantaged when implementing regulations. It is not in the interest of national governments to enforce unduly restrictive policies. This makes country-specific regulation unattractive. Therefore, there is the need for stringent and long-term-focused global regulation. However, the question still is whether international climate policies will remain in their established policy direction or move forward as far as it is necessary. The difficulty in reaching agreement was demonstrated at Kyoto, and again at Copenhagen and Cancun. We conclude that because of the global nature of the solutions required, solving them on the political level is exceedingly difficult. There is no single obvious perpetrator, no individual state whose actions ought to be targeted and changed and, given the economic sacrifices required, no state is willing to take the initial step. This is strikingly similar to the financial crisis, and definitely deserves further thought (see Chapter 9).

## Distortion of intra-generational equities

One striking phenomenon of both crises is that poorer individuals and nations are most likely to suffer as they do not have the same access to coping mechanisms as the rich do. In the US, it was the low-income, subprime mortgage holders who were the first and hardest hit by the economic crisis; unable to keep up payments, many lost their homes. Individuals who were unemployed or who had limited savings were also in an extremely vulnerable position. With a fall in commodity prices and the credit crunch, global investment was scaled back, causing capital to become scarcer. The decline in private capital flows caused many nations to be hit hard by the downturns in Europe and the US. This was particularly devastating for developing nations. The global lack of investment activities put them in a situation of continuing recession. The World Bank (2009) recently stated that developing countries face increasingly grave prospects if the dramatic deterioration in their capital inflows from exports, remittances, and foreign direct investment is not reversed in 2010. For example, in Thailand GDP dropped by a fifth in the last quarter of 2008 (World Bank 2009). As discussed in Chapter 7, the same

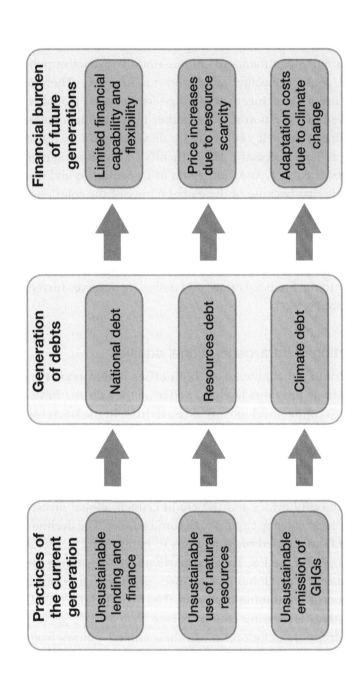

Figure 10 The creation of debt

holds for the carbon crisis—poorer individuals and nations will suffer the most.

### Distortion of inter-generational equities

Both crises create debt (see Fig. 10). This means that the current generation seeks to postpone the negative consequences of unsustainable behavior into the future. In the financial crisis this unsustainable behavior is apparent in the creation of huge national debt. Governments provided tremendous amounts of money for industry and the banking system in order to prevent a serious global recession. They incentivized increased levels of consumption to spur economic growth through programs such as the "cash-for-clunkers" in the US. These efforts were founded on the creation of higher levels of national debt. Unsustainable behavior in light of the carbon crisis can be argued in a similar way. With respect to the input dimension, the depletion of natural resources—in our context notably fossil fuels—creates a resources debt. Future generations will have to bear this debt in terms of higher prices for the resources; cheap fossil-fuel-based energy will not be available for later generations. With respect to the output dimension, the current generation is causing a climate debt. Stemming from the accumulation of greenhouse gases in the atmosphere, climate change will further intensify and future generations will have to bear the negative consequences. These will become concrete through the cost of adaptation measures.

## Differences between the crises

The purpose of this chapter is to illustrate what we can learn from the financial crisis in order to manage the carbon crisis better. The parallels identified above illustrate similar traps and patterns in both crises. Despite these parallels, there are some significant differences between the two crises, which are important for understanding the scope of the carbon crisis. First, the pace of the responses of decision makers has been markedly different in both crises. Action taken against the financial crisis was quick to follow the initial identification of problems. For example, two weeks after Lehman Brothers collapsed, the US government passed a $700 billion bank bailout plan. All major countries undertook similar efforts. In contrast, the Kyoto Protocol, a key response to climate change, came into force 12 years after the subject was first broached at the Rio Earth Summit in 1992. The same slow pace can be observed in more recent climate efforts: the main result of the most important post-Kyoto meeting—the 15th United Nations Climate Change Conference in late 2009 in Copenhagen—is that there was no real result that addresses the sources of the problem. The follow-up meeting one year later in Cancun did not change this situation significantly. Thus, there is a big difference in terms of both political will and ability to respond to the emerging carbon crisis.

Second, the main effects of the financial crisis are likely to be resolved within the next five to ten years, while the carbon crisis has a much more long-term dimension. The financial crisis can be addressed now, by taking actions such as reversing the cash flow freeze imposed by banks, creating more effective regulation and financial mechanisms. As such, its effects are limited to the short and mid term (although there will also be long-term problems owing to the national debts created). Despite the precarious option of geo-engineering, which we will discuss later on, the environmental damage caused by climate change cannot be reversed in the short to medium term. How and whether the temperature increase can be reversed in the long term is yet to be determined and it is even more uncertain whether the damages and changes in ecological systems can be reversed, and if so how. Humanity therefore will have to adapt fairly dramatically and in costly ways (financially and in lives lost) to climate change.

Third, it is important to acknowledge the different short- and long-term causal relationships: interventions on financial markets usually yield immediate consequences. Through a joint effort of all major governments globally, it was possible to mitigate a global recession. Radical reductions in greenhouse gases, however, will take decades to become tangible because of a time lag between greenhouse gas emissions and their warming effects in the atmosphere. The temperature increases that are currently being experienced are due to the accelerated emission levels over the last 200 years (Wigley 2005). Even a stabilization of atmospheric concentrations of greenhouse gases would lead to continued warming and only if any further carbon dioxide emissions could be fully eliminated, would temperatures stabilize or even decrease over time (Matthews and Weaver 2010).

## Wrapping it up: what are the key lessons?

There are many parallels between the financial and the carbon crisis. The main lesson is: similar to the financial crisis, the carbon crisis would have broad and severe implications for humanity as well as businesses. However, we cannot reverse the effects of climate change and fossil fuel scarcity as easily as we can repair the global financial system. Therefore, tackling the issues early enough is even more important in the carbon crisis context. But looking at the world today, the question is: are we unwilling to solve these problems because of the difficulties they entail?

It seems that we are unwilling to use the knowledge that we have about potential crises. Prior to the financial crisis there were many warnings and also detailed knowledge. Based on earlier financial crises in Mexico, the Far East, Russia, and Brazil, Stephen Valdez (2000) discusses the sources, consequences, and potential solutions of global financial turmoil. This was discussed in the chapter "Global Financial Crises" in the third edition of his book *An Introduction to Global Financial Markets*. Studying the fifth edition of the book (Valdez 2007), this chapter is missing. Are these insights redundant as no decision maker will use the information anyway? Do we in fact need financial crises to renew our economies in a Schumpeter's logic of creative destruction?

Looking backwards in history, financial crises have usually had the potential to trigger considerable change and innovation. For example, the economic collapse in Europe after the Second World War resulted in the development of the Marshall Plan, which eventually revived Europe economically. The current financial crisis will likely help restructure the global economy and reduce the surplus of production capacities in areas such as the automotive industry.

In a similar manner it can be argued that fossil fuel scarcity, which will drive high oil and energy prices, may foster the transition from fossil fuels to renewable energy sources. We would like to emphasize the negative consequences of such an adjustment process for poorer individuals, especially for those living in developing nations. Nevertheless, it seems that perhaps it will take high prices for fossil-fuel-based energy to trigger the necessary change towards a low-carbon future. For climate change, however, this process may not work. Once the Earth experiences severe negative effects of climate change, it will be too late to take countermeasures. Using Schumpeter's approach of creative destruction will not work in the climate change context: the damages are partly irreversible and there will be no creative phase following the destruction. It is essential that we use the information from climate science and other environmental crises (Shrivastava 1992) and base our strategies on what we know today.

We conclude that a farsighted analysis and precautionary management—which has to start now—is needed. We suggest two key mechanisms for an accelerated path towards a low-carbon society: substantial action via adequate political enforcement on the macro level and voluntary action-driven carbon reduction initiatives on the meso and micro level. As derived in Chapter 1, both actions have to focus on two key technological challenges: the decoupling of economic growth and energy demand and the decarbonization of the energy mix.

# 9
# Macro level
## Industrial policies for climate change

Over the course of the financial crisis there has been an interest-ing mix of pessimism and optimism regarding the likelihood of a carbon crisis. Many people are concerned that climate change is being overshadowed by the financial crisis while others argue that a reduction in economic activity is needed to stabilize and ultimately reduce carbon dioxide emissions. Therefore, should we be embrac-ing this financial crisis, allowing industrial downturn and reduc-tion in spending, so as to save our planet? We believe in a different approach and view the current situation as a unique opportunity to bring about much-needed change in the global economic system in order to mitigate climate damage and secure future energy supply. This chapter takes a macro-level perspective and investigates poten-tial options for industrial policies that are important in this context.

To this end, we would like to emphasize two important aspects. First, without any countermeasures, both climate change and fossil fuel scarcity are very likely to harm the global economy. Second, we have the knowledge of renewable energy and low-carbon technolo-gies in order to curb emissions and reduce our carbon dependency. Therefore, the key question for industrial policies is how the cur-rent locked-in position can be overcome and diffusion of clean low-carbon technologies can be accelerated on a global scale? We cannot claim to fully answer this question—this would be beyond the scope of this book. Instead, we highlight two central issues of current climate policy efforts: the lack of stringency and the lack of financing. Furthermore, we elaborate on the idea of creating a global carbon-equal fund as one promising way of overcoming these issues.

## (Global) Climate policy: the solution?

Many countries have established climate change and energy-related regulations and policies: for example, greenhouse gas reporting programs, regional emission trading schemes, carbon and energy taxes, and carbon reduction and energy efficiency programs (see Table 7). However, individual governments alone cannot resolve climate change. Action taken only by a few countries will not stop climate change if other countries continue to emit or even increase their emissions. But individual governments will not implement stringent regulations because of competitiveness concerns. For example, if a single national government implemented new regulations that would significantly constrain its own national businesses with carbon taxes or emission cuts, companies—notably global players—would immediately consider outsourcing their production to other countries with less stringent legislation. This phenomenon is known as "carbon leakage." Therefore, there is a clear need for new industrial policies that aim at global carbon reduction and simultaneously create a level playing field.

Table 7 **Selected climate change and energy-related regulations and policies**

Source: based on Kolk and Hoffmann 2007, Pew Center on Global Climate Change,[1] and official government web pages

| Geography | Legislation name | Short description | Time period |
|-----------|------------------|-------------------|-------------|
| Australia | National Greenhouse and Energy Reporting Act 2007 (NGER) | Provides for the reporting and dissemination of information related to companies' greenhouse gas emissions at specified quantities per financial year. Key objective is to underpin the future Australian Carbon Pollution Reduction Scheme (CPRS), providing the data on which future obligations will be based | First annual reporting in July 2008 |
| | Carbon Pollution Reduction Scheme (CPRS) | Part of the Australian Government's strategy to reduce Australia's carbon pollution by 60 percent of 2000 levels by 2050. Not all corporations that report under existing NGER legislation will be subject to CPRS obligations | The Australian Government has delayed introduction of the CPRS until after the current Kyoto Protocol commitment ends in 2012 |
| | Energy Efficiency Opportunities | Requires large companies using more than 0.5 petajoules (PJ) of energy per year to identify, evaluate, and report publicly on cost-effective energy savings opportunities | First annual reporting in 2008 |
| | Greenhouse Gas Reduction Scheme | New South Wales state level mandatory cap-and-trade system | Start 2003 |

1 www.pewclimate.org/what_s_being_done/in_the_states/regional_initiatives.cfm (accessed February 28, 2011).

| Geography | Legislation name | Short description | Time period |
|---|---|---|---|
| Australia *(cont.)* | Victorian Energy Efficiency Target (VEET) Act 2007 | Legally obliges larger energy retailers to conduct household-level energy saving programs through the creation, acquisition, and surrender of Victorian energy efficiency certificates | Start 2009 |
| Canada | Greenhouse Gas Emissions Reporting Program | Requires all facilities that emit the equivalent of 100,000 tonnes of greenhouse gases and above to submit a report | Start 2004 |
| | Western Climate Initiative (WCI) | An initiative—started by states and provinces along the western rim of North America (British Columbia, Manitoba, Ontario, and Quebec)—to combat climate change caused by global warming, independent of their national governments. It identifies, evaluates and implements ways to collectively reduce greenhouse gas emissions | In 2007, the WCI set a goal of reducing greenhouse gas emissions by 15 percent from 2005 levels by 2020 |
| European Union | EU Emissions Trading Scheme | Includes all EU countries (27) plus Norway, Iceland, and Lichtenstein. The Scheme covers about 40 percent of EU carbon dioxide emissions from over 10,000 facilities. Phase I was considered a trial phase. Phase II imposes tighter restrictions, as well as selected auctioning of allowances instead of distributing them freely | Phase I: 2005–2007  Phase II: 2008–12  Phase III: 2013–20 |
| Germany | Renewable Energy Act | Incentivizes the use and development of renewable energy through a feed-in tariff scheme in order to increase the amount of renewable energy within the power supply in Germany | Introduced in 2000. Latest version of this Act came into force in 2009 |

| Geography | Legislation name | Short description | Time period |
|---|---|---|---|
| Italy and France | Tradable White Certificate (TWC) Scheme | Requires market actors, generally retail energy suppliers or distributors, to meet government-mandated targets for energy savings. This is achieved through the introduction of energy saving measures, either in all sectors or more specifically in the residential arena. Suppliers exceeding or undercutting their objectives can trade energy savings certificates as required for compliance | Start 2005 (Italy) and 2006 (France) |
| New Zealand | New Zealand Emissions Trading Scheme | Introduces a price on greenhouse gas emissions to encourage the reduction of emissions and the planting of forests to absorb carbon dioxide. The NZ ETS is the system in which New Zealand Units (NZUs) are traded. Effectively, one NZU is the right to emit one ton of greenhouse gases. It includes all sectors of the economy and all greenhouse gases by 2015, it is internationally linked, and employs self-assessment for monitoring, reporting, and verifying emissions | Start 2009 |
| Spain | Plan de Energías Renovables 2005–2010 | Sets a renewable energy goal of 12 percent of total energy consumption for 2010. Capacity targets for 2010 are as follows: wind (20,155 MW), photovoltaic (400 MW), solar thermal (4.9 million m$^2$), solar thermal electric (500 MW), and biomass (1,695 MW). Support mechanisms in place to achieve this include a feed-in tariff system, low interest loans to incentivize investment, and a fuel tax exemption on biofuels | To be achieved within the period 2005–10 |

| Geography | Legislation name | Short description | Time period |
|---|---|---|---|
| Spain *(cont.)* | Plan de Energías Renovables 2011–2020 | Sets binding targets, minimum requirements, and specific technology goals following the assessment period 2005–10 in order to reach Spain's target of receiving 20 percent of the energy supply from renewable energy sources. The rules governing this plan are to be contained within the Law on Energy Efficiency and Renewable Energy (in development) | 2011–20 |
| Switzerland | The $CO_2$ Act | The $CO_2$ Act's objective is to reduce the emission of carbon dioxide arising from the combustion of fossil fuels by 10 percent versus the 1990 level by 2010. The Act comprises the Swiss carbon dioxide tax and emissions trading scheme. The scheme allows companies to engage in voluntary emission reduction, allowing them to participate in emissions trading and exempting them from the carbon dioxide tax | Start 2000<br>Taxation: 2008–12<br>Voluntary trading: 2009 |
| United Kingdom | Carbon Reduction Commitment | Reduces the level of carbon emissions currently produced by the larger "low energy-intensive" organizations by approximately 1.2 million tonnes of carbon dioxide per year by 2020. As a Climate Change Bill commitment, the scheme is aiming for a 60 percent reduction in carbon dioxide emissions by 2050. It is also a mandatory emissions trading scheme targeting large commercial and public sector organizations using more than 6,000 MWh/yr of electricity | Start 2010 |

| Geography | Legislation name | Short description | Time period |
|---|---|---|---|
| United Kingdom (cont.) | Climate Change Act 2008 | Introduces a legally binding target of an 80 percent reduction in greenhouse gas emissions by 2050 against a 1990 baseline. A key provision of this Act is the introduction of a carbon budgeting system which caps emissions over 5-year periods | The first three carbon budgets will run from 2008–12, 2013–17, and 2018–22 |
| United States of America | EPA mandatory reporting rule | Demands US-wide mandatory yearly reporting for firms emitting above 25,000 tons carbon dioxide per year of direct emissions, including 13,000 facilities | Became effective in 2009 |
| | American Clean Energy and Security Act 2009 | Sets forth provisions concerning clean energy, energy efficiency, reducing global warming pollution, transitioning to a clean energy economy, and providing for agriculture and forestry-related offsets. It includes the provision of establishing a cap-and-trade system for greenhouse gas emissions and setting goals for reducing such emissions from covered sources by 83 percent of 2005 levels by 2050 | The bill was passed in the House of Representatives in June 2009 but was later stopped by the Senate. Of this writing, it is not clear if it will be revived |
| | California Climate Action Registry | A private non-profit organization set up by the State of California which promotes the greenhouse gas reporting. Its over 300 members voluntarily measure, verify, and publicly report their greenhouse gas emissions | Formed 2001, first reporting 2002; after 2009 reports must be made to the Climate Registry |

| Geography | Legislation name | Short description | Time period |
|---|---|---|---|
| United States of America (cont.) | The California Global Warming Solutions Act of 2006 | Sets a 2020 greenhouse gas emissions reduction goal into law. It directed the California Air Resources Board to begin developing discrete early actions to reduce greenhouse gases while also preparing a scoping plan to identify how best to reach the 2020 limit. The reduction measures to meet the 2020 target are to be adopted by the start of 2011 | Reporting started 2009; cap and trade start 2012 |
| | Midwestern Greenhouse Gas Reduction Accord | Establishes the Midwestern Greenhouse Gas Reduction Program, which aims to establish emission targets and time frames consistent with signing states' targets while developing a market-based and multi-sector cap-and-trade mechanism to help achieve those reduction targets. Nine Midwestern governors and two Canadian premiers have signed on to participate or observe in the accord | First reporting 2009; trading starting 2012 |
| | Regional Greenhouse Gas Initiative (RGGI) | Aims to reduce 10 percent of emissions relative to 2009 until 2018 through a cap-and-trade program. Includes ten US states (Connecticut, Delaware, Maine, Maryland, Massachusetts, New Hampshire, New Jersey, New York, Rhode Island, and Vermont) and is mandatory for electricity power generators which are 25 MW or greater in size | Trading started 2009 (first compliance period 2009–11) |

| Geography | Legislation name | Short description | Time period |
|---|---|---|---|
| United States of America (*cont.*) | Western Climate Initiative | Aims to reduce economy-wide greenhouse gas emissions by 15 percent below 2005 levels by 2020 through a cap-and-trade system. Includes seven US States (Arizona, California, Montana, New Mexico, Oregon, Utah, and Washington) and four Canadian provinces (British Columbia, Manitoba, Ontario, and Quebec) and covers the electricity, industry, and transportation sectors and residential and commercial fuel use amounting to around 90 percent of emissions in those states | Start 2012 (reporting 2010) |
| | Energy Security and Climate Stewardship Platform for the Midwest | Aims for energy efficiency improvements, low-carbon transportation fuel availability, renewable electricity production, and carbon capture and storage development. In November 2007, the Governors of eleven Midwestern states and the Premier of one Canadian province individually adopted all or portions of an Energy Security and Climate Stewardship Platform | Regional regulatory framework for carbon capture and storage by 2010<br><br>All new coal plants in the region intend to capture and store carbon dioxide by 2020 |

The most important question with respect to international climate policy is: Why is it so difficult for the world's nations to agree on a global climate treaty? For example, there were no such difficulties when agreeing on the Montreal Protocol for the phase-out of chlorofluorocarbons in response to the depletion of the ozone layer. This was possible since there were substitutes at hand for chlorofluorocarbons and there were fewer involved participants. Substituting carbon on the other hand is not that easy. Therefore, the Kyoto Protocol has to be regarded as a great success. Although its effectiveness in terms of dramatic emission reductions is questionable, it was the first time that the majority of the world's nations committed to a global climate treaty. Compared with that, however, the outcome of the Copenhagen conference in 2009 was rather discouraging; some authors even considered it the crash of international climate policy (Prins *et al.* 2010). As the UN Conference as a whole simply "took note" of the Copenhagen Accord, the targets and actions will not be binding and the accord will only have an informal status within the UN system. One small step was taken at the UN Conference in Cancun in 2010: the outcome was an agreement adopted by the involved parties that global average temperature should be kept below two degrees Celsius above pre-industrial levels and that urgent action is required to meet this long-term goal. However, no agreement was reached on how to extend the Kyoto Protocol, how to initiate a potential green climate fund, or how emission reduction targets could be set. As no effective multinational agreement has been reached, the question is how the mounting issue of climate change can be addressed—especially in the short term. Thus, greater levels of more globally coordinated actions are necessary to prevent the repetition of past mistakes within the negotiation processes. For example, the focus could be laid on more "local" action by integrating communities, municipalities, and counties or states. This is an understandably difficult task, but it is necessary to have some form of global agreement on how to manage the carbon crisis.

It is essential to acknowledge the importance of further fostering global climate policy efforts. But top-down climate policy efforts have their limits as they are based on the mainstream economic assumption that agents are perfectly rational (Marechal and Lazaric

2010). Furthermore, such policies often underestimated institutional complexities (Rayner 2010). As a consequence, important aspects cannot be grasped, which could explain why we remain in a "carbon-locked-in" position (Unruh 2000); for example, path-dependency of technological change, habits of firms and consumers, organizational inertia, and psychologically rooted non-economic barriers (Marechal and Lazaric 2010). Owing to these limits, we agree with other researchers (e.g., Prins *et al.* 2010) that a significant reframing in policy direction is required if we are seriously intending to accelerate our steps towards a low-carbon society. We are aware of the huge debate and the sheer volume of proposals and ideas involved in the international climate change debate. It is not our intention to add further detail to this debate. Instead, we would like to critically reflect on certain developments and point to some promising solutions. Many political issues, conflicts of interest, and other aspects may be discussed regarding the stagnation of international climate negotiations. Depending on individual perspectives and background, one may be favored over the other. From an industrial policy perspective, we highlight two central issues: the lack of stringency and financing. We strongly believe future negotiations and climate policy efforts could benefit from a significant change in policy direction in a manner that adequately reflects those two issues.

## The lack of stringency

One central issue of previous international climate policy efforts was that proliferation of new approaches, ideas, and advances added further complexity to the already complex debate. Every lobby group, government, and interest group sought to push forward its own agenda and interests. As a consequence there were a huge number of opinions, exceptions and papers on how best to save the planet. In this flurry of initiatives people lost sight of the main objective: *significant* greenhouse gas reductions. As a consequence, worldwide emissions are persistently rising, currently at a rate close to 3 percent per annum (Rayner 2010). In addition, all major established political climate frameworks were subject to uncertainty. For example, the Kyoto Protocol officially ends in 2012. What happens then? The European Union's Emissions Trading Scheme has different trading periods with different rules and mechanisms. Why is there no consistency? In this situation of increasing complexity and uncertainty, one main outcome is: a lack of stringency in climate policy. The best example is the outcomes of recent years in international climate policy, with its (negative) peak in Copenhagen. Instead, especially from an industry perspective, what was needed was the establishment of a stringent climate change governance system that follows simple rules, sets a predictable framework, and is easy to understand.

Lack of stringency is not only attributed to ineffective international political processes but can also be illustrated by policy schemes that have already been implemented. The most far-reaching regulation on the international level is the European Union's Emissions Trading Scheme, which was established in 2005 covering more than 12,000 installations in the EU member states. It is not necessary to describe in detail the mechanisms of this scheme, as there are numerous sources that serve this purpose very well: for example, the official web page of the European Union.[1] Starting with the positive, this system is a clear achievement: major industrial greenhouse gas emitters are covered by the trading scheme, including electricity generation and heavy industries. As a "trading" scheme it follows a market and economic logic. Emissions are reduced where it is least expensive to do so. Another clear advantage is it establishes a clear price for carbon. As only limited allowances are given to the participants, companies that need more allowances have to buy them from other companies. On the downside the trading scheme is a prime example of how complexity and uncertainty can yield a lack of stringency.

The trading scheme bears many examples of sources of complexity: every government within the European Union decides on its own about the allocation of the allowances; there are different trading periods with different conditions; there are specific rules on how companies may use Certified Emission Reductions issued by projects within the Clean Development Mechanism, and so on. Owing to the sheer number of rules, exceptions, and conditions, the scheme

---

1   ec.europa.eu/environment/climat/emission/index_en.htm (accessed February 28, 2011).

is only understood by experts in this area. Furthermore, all these aspects are inherently subject to uncertainty, as the specific mechanisms and regulations change over time, so there is, in addition, a lot of regulatory uncertainty (Engau and Hoffmann 2009; Hoffmann *et al.* 2009).

In this complex and unpredictable situation the first trading period of the European Union's Emissions Trading Scheme (2005–2007) created the ground for some interesting developments. For example, the caps on emissions were set "far too high, primarily because of the failure of European Union member states to resist the lobbying efforts of powerful vested interests" (UNDP 2007: 11). As a consequence, there was a serious drifting down of prices at the end of the first period. Nevertheless, the scheme created a market and pricing mechanism for carbon dioxide. Although allowances for carbon dioxide emissions were given free of charge to market participants as a basic rule (this is usually referred to as "grandfathering"), the scheme established a carbon price—at least at the beginning of the first period. Some companies considered the price as an opportunity cost. That is, even though they needed their (free) allocated allowances for their own emissions, they sold them on the market and generated additional revenues. Companies priced in some artificial costs into their accounts to cover their carbon exposure and raised prices, which simply generated more profits for them. This phenomenon is referred to as "windfall profits." Such windfall profits were realized by many European energy utilities. As a result, electricity prices went up and customers had to bear the artificial cost of emissions trading. But beyond that, a recent review of existing research on the European Union's Emissions Trading Scheme has shown that influence of the scheme on firms in the energy sector has been fairly low (Zhang and Wei 2010). In addition, there was an over-allocation of allowances to emitters and a high volatility in allowance prices, which can be ascribed to deficient design and implementation of the scheme (Ellerman and Buchner 2008; Ellerman and Joskow 2008).

With respect to the overall effectiveness of the system, the first trading period (2005–2007) is questionable. The *verified* emissions allowances of all firms increased very slightly from 2,014 million tons of carbon dioxide in 2005 to 2,052 million tons of carbon dioxide in 2007 (Anderson and Maria 2010). Of course, proponents of the scheme argue that it was just a trial period. But in light of the urgency to find adequate answers to the mounting issue of climate change and the indisputable responsibility of industrialized countries in this regard, three years was a long trial. In addition, there is already an indication that the second trading period (2008–2012) will not be more effective, further questioning the stringency of the scheme (Morris and Worthington 2010).

In conclusion, we suggest some important changes in policy direction. In order to foster the stringency of climate policy, special industrial policies are required that seek to reduce complexity and uncertainty. We need clear and predictable legislation and easy to implement climate regulations that target emission reductions. Such a stringent policy system should not be targeted primarily at constraining businesses. Instead, it sets the basic boundaries and conditions for low-carbon production patterns, while progressing in a predictable and reliable manner via clear long-term targets. It is important for businesses to be able to integrate climate policy into their strategic planning. Short-term readjustments and quick-fix solutions result in suboptimal (financial) outcomes. For example, a coal-fired power plant that is built today has a payback period of about 30–40 years. In light of the climate challenge, it is now political consensus in Germany that coal subsidies will fade out. Coal will become a much more expensive source for electricity production and it is likely that production plants will need to be shut down before being fully amortized. This predictable and reliable condition regarding the future of coal may be the reason why, currently, some big energy companies in Germany have stopped their plans for constructing new coal-fired utilities.

# The lack of financing

In recent years, no country, according to the World Bank, has been able to substantially reduce poverty and sustain economic growth rates without substantially increasing its use of energy (Haughton and Khandker 2009). Energy is therefore critical in maintaining and expanding economies. This being the one main objective of governments, especially with regard to the financial crisis, fostering investments in clean energy technologies would therefore be an ideal long-term investment opportunity—in developing as well as developed countries. Not only are investments in low-carbon infrastructure and technologies focusing on energy efficiency, transportation, and renewable resources environmentally beneficial, they also have the potential to create new jobs. As such, investments in renewable energy technologies seem to have the potential to boost economic growth: "All countries stand to gain from $CO_2$ mitigation. Unfortunately, the world currently lacks a credible mechanism for unlocking this win–win scenario" (UNDP 2007: 12). The question then is: why don't we accelerate such investments to an extent and pace that is needed?

From an industrial policies point of view the answer is simple. There is a significant lack of financing mechanisms required to get such investments off the ground. Of course, there are plenty of examples of how individual companies may generate win–win situations by increasing their energy efficiency. In such cases, they reduce their energy use and thus related greenhouse gas emissions while simultaneously reducing the costs of purchasing energy. In such situations companies—once having realized how to reap these low-hanging fruits—do invest in required technologies and process improvements. However, the bulk of investments in renewable energy technologies, improved infrastructure, and low-carbon production processes may not result in immediate win–win situations. Some may require upfront investments and the payoffs are rather long-term. Furthermore, many energy-related investments have long payback periods. Therefore, many firms may be in some kind of path-dependent situation as previous carbon-intensive investments are not yet fully paid back. For firms in developing economies in particular, the necessity for upfront investments may be one key obstacle: such investments do not occur pervasively because of a lack of sufficient financial resources. As a result, companies remain in their "carbon-locked-in" situation if no adequate incentives are set. In order to overcome this situation, industrial policies are required that establish financing mechanisms. These can fulfill different purposes: even out additional costs for individual companies; enable start-up funding; and foster international knowledge transfer.

In conclusion, we therefore suggest that future climate policy direction should put more emphasis on the details of how to finance future efforts towards a low-carbon society. In order to foster investments in low-carbon technologies, climate policy should seek to establish industrial policies that are focused on enabling and incentivizing local action and accelerating the required knowledge transfer. Obviously, a key question is: Who should pay for this and who will benefit from the money? In the following we elaborate on the creation of a global carbon-equal fund that could serve as a financing mechanism.

## Creation of a global carbon-equal fund

From an inter-generational equity perspective it is important to note that industrialized countries already have a very high carbon footprint, measured in terms of the amount of carbon dioxide emitted per capita. If we imagine a situation where industrialized countries reduced their carbon footprints overnight, climate change would no longer be such a large issue—at least in the near future. However, with developing countries using and emitting more and more carbon in the long term it would only be a matter of time before the problem returns. This is why we need both management of emissions occurring in the industrialized world as well as strategies that prevent developing countries from growing in the same carbon-intensive way. Furthermore, as climate change is already the reality, there needs to be greater global consensus on how to manage and finance necessary adaptation. This requires the rich to provide support to the poor who are struggling to cope with a problem that is not of their own making.

One possible solution is the creation of a global carbon-equal fund and, indeed, a key outcome of the recent UN Climate Change Conference in Cancun was the agreement to establish a "Green Climate Fund." It seems that international climate policy is still moving forward, which is most needed and welcome. However, important details still need to be discussed and agreed (compare, for example, the Oxford Energy and Environment Brief from January 2011; Harmeling and Müller 2011). Notably, it is not yet clear how the money for the fund will be raised. Our suggestion of a global carbon-equal fund is based on the idea that nations would have to agree on a global price for carbon emissions and an emission threshold per capita. Each individual person with emissions above this threshold would pay the carbon price per ton above the threshold. Persons below the threshold have no financial burden. We leave it up to experts to discuss what such a potential threshold should be based on. One option, for example, could be the total global emissions required to stabilize the climate at the objective of two degrees Celsius, divided by the global population. However, our key message here is: keep it simple and establish one global carbon price that every human being has to pay if his or her carbon footprint is above a certain maximum. The only, but surely difficult, task for international climate policy then would be to agree on the price per ton of carbon and the threshold. Individual countries would be responsible for paying the money into the fund. It should also be their responsibility to decide how to charge the money and which kinds of incentive they internally set for companies and individuals to reduce their carbon footprint. As such, at this level no international climate policy solutions are required.

Such a fund would set a carbon price signal that incentivizes countries in the developed world to emit less per person and developing countries to avoid crossing the threshold. Of course for such an approach, many details need to be discussed and agreed upon. For example, how to deal with fuel subsidies (particularly in the US), where governance structures are required, and which institutional settings are necessary and most adequate.

An interesting option could follow a carbon tax system that is based on the concept of a value-added tax. Such a tax is considered to be a consumption tax; that is, a surcharge, usually a certain percentage, is added to the market value of a product or service. In a similar manner to the market value, a carbon emission factor per product can be determined. Many carbon footprint initiatives and labels already follow such an idea. Central to this tax would be that the carbon tax of each stage of its manufacture or distribution would ultimately be passed on to the consumer. Thus, there would be fewer negative effects for business in terms of additional costs or reduced competitiveness compared with foreign companies. Of course, the implementation of such a carbon tax would require further agreements and clarifications, such as determining the exact carbon footprint or how to deal with imported goods. Nevertheless, in sum, a carbon tax can be assumed to result into two main effects. First, consumers would become aware of their carbon footprint stemming from individual products and services and seek to reduce it. Second, companies would try to reduce their carbon loading throughout the supply chain in order to offer competitive products with lower carbon taxes.

We would like to further illustrate the idea of the carbon fund in combination with the carbon tax using an example. Assuming as the outcome of international negotiations countries agreed on a carbon price of $25 per ton—which is at the lower end of current prices for offsetting one ton of greenhouse gas emissions on the voluntary carbon market—and the threshold at 2 tons per capita per year. This would correspond to $535 per annum per person in the US.[2] This of course is an average value. Depending on the carbon loading of the individual lifestyle as determined by the carbon tax on products and services, individuals would pay more or less than this average value. In sum, the US government would generate $176 billion income from the tax. This is about 1.2 percent of US GDP, which roughly corresponds to Stern's (Stern 2006) estimation of 1 percent of global GDP required for stabilization at 500–550 ppm carbon dioxide equivalents (respectively at a two degrees Celsius temperature increase).

Besides setting incentives for carbon reductions, the main objective of the fund would not be to formulate and reinforce emissions targets for individual countries. Instead, the money gathered by the

2 This number is based on the year 2008 when the US emitted 7,052 million tons carbon dioxide equivalents (www.eia.doe.gov/oiaf/1605/ggrpt/#total, accessed March 1, 2011) and had an official population of 301,621,157 (www.infoplease.com/ipa/A0004986.html, accessed March 1, 2011). This corresponds to 23.4 tons carbon dioxide equivalents per capita (this is higher than the US result shown in Figure 7 in Chapter 7; that figure refers only to carbon dioxide emissions). Subtracting 2 tons (the threshold) from 23.4 tons and multiplying it by $25 per ton yields $535.

fund should be used to establish a global climate policy system that enables and incentivizes local action, knowledge sharing, and technology transfer for both climate mitigation and adaptation. We discuss this special nexus between mitigation and adaptation in more detail in the last chapter of this book. Regarding the functioning of the fund, developed countries would repay parts of their resource and climate debts: for example, by providing developing countries with the necessary funding and technology to adapt to climate change. In order to best implement industrial policies for climate change based on inter- and intra-generational equity principles, we suggest three central ways in which the financing mechanisms of the fund could work: the foundation of local climate agencies; the implementation of sectoral approaches; and the fostering of low-carbon entrepreneurship.

## Foundation of local climate agencies

Many companies may see the need and also the advantage of increasing their carbon efficiency. We discuss this in more detail in Chapter 11. However, many companies remain in a "carbon-locked-in" position (Unruh 2000). Many individual reasons may be found for this, usually high upfront costs or a lack of knowledge are at least part of the problem. In order to reach and support companies, the foundation of local agencies is important, which could work under the umbrella of a Climate Change Mitigation Facility as proposed by the United Nations Development Programme (UNDP 2007). Such agencies should assess the feasibility and efficacy of projects and manage the allocation of the financing aid. Of course such assessments require a great deal of knowledge and expertise, of which much has been gained already in the context of the Clean Development Mechanism and already established local energy and environmental agencies, for example the Effizienz-Agentur NRW[3] in Germany. Founded in 1998, the purpose of this agency is to encourage local firms to adopt comprehensive strategic and technical improvements that reflect the objective of a sustainable economy. Based on a team of more than 20 consultants, the agency transfers knowledge, offers

3  www.efanrw.de (accessed March 1, 2011).

concrete financial advantages, and helps firms to progress into the future through new strategies, innovative technology, and ecologically oriented measures. Such efforts could be copied globally. Nevertheless, such agencies would have to deal with several trade-offs. For example, some biofuels may compete with land use and food supply; electricity powered cars require a low-carbon electricity mix to be effective; wind turbines require a significant amount of cement, which is very carbon-intensive during production. Therefore, one of the key challenges would be the establishment of a database/knowledge network on how to best handle such trade-off situations.

Beyond focusing on companies in industrialized countries with high levels of greenhouse gas emissions, the climate agencies in developing countries should focus on helping companies in areas such as rural electrification, sustainable agriculture, and water conservation. As such, the fund would be the prime vehicle for industrialized countries to help developing nations to subsidize such firms. This would prevent further carbon emissions, enable growth and production, and help with adaptation measures for climate change. Notably the latter seems important: beyond climate mitigation, the agencies may also use the money raised by the fund in order to finance a variety of adaptation projects—in the developed and developing world. This is a key area for urgent action as:

> the international response on adaptation has fallen far short of what is required. Several dedicated multilateral financing mechanisms have been created, including the Least Developed Country Fund and the Special Climate Change Fund. Delivery through these mechanisms has been limited (UNDP 2007: 14).

We acknowledge that a transparent and reliable governance system is required in order to establish a fair allocation of the money between countries. The political negotiation regarding such a system may be difficult. The main objective thus should be to establish a non-complex system based on inter-generational and intra-generational equity principles.

## Implementation of sectoral approaches

In addition to the establishment of such climate agencies, the sharing of technology and knowledge especially in carbon-intensive industries should be targeted by special industrial policies. Individual countries usually avoid taking significant action with regard to industry for fear of becoming economically isolated and disadvantaged. The aim of the so-called sectoral approach is to introduce a global policy targeted at specific industries. The common idea behind sectoral approaches is that new policies on climate change mitigation can be based on sectoral considerations, which take into account specific circumstances and conditions for greenhouse gas reductions of one individual or several industries (Baron 2006). The recent discussion about sectoral approaches is centered on how an industry sector could come to an agreement to initiate action towards greenhouse gas reductions. As this is the one central focus of the debate, we briefly summarize the discussion.

One important aspect of sectoral approaches is the question of how to set emission reduction targets. These can be binding or non-binding: binding targets are a legal obligation to meet a certain target for all involved parties, whereas non-binding targets do not impose any consequences in the case of non-compliance. Furthermore, a mixture of target setting approaches can be adopted: for example, companies from developed countries have to meet binding targets whereas companies from developing countries agree to voluntary, non-binding targets (so-called "no-lose pledges"). Companies in developed countries could be incentivized to adopt such targets if, for example, emissions reductions below an agreed baseline could be sold in an international carbon market.

Sectoral approaches have certain advantages. Given that sectoral approaches cover major parts of an industrial sector on a global level, they reduce the impacts on competitiveness of nationally based emissions regulations. Notably, they reduce the likelihood of "carbon leakage," a phenomenon discussed above (Felder and Rutherford 1993). With effective global sectoral approaches in place, companies have no reason to relocate carbon-intense processes to countries where emission regulation is less stringent. Moreover, sectoral approaches based on no-lose pledges could serve to break a potential deadlock in international negotiations. Furthermore, such approaches can improve data and information on developing countries' emissions performance, a critical factor in determining technology needs in those countries. This is a key requirement for raising awareness of benchmark performance and broadens the application of best available technologies.

However, sectoral approaches also face certain limitations and, therefore, the effective implementation of such approaches has to address the following: sectoral approaches usually seek to provide a level playing field by ensuring the participation of major companies worldwide through the use of benchmarking systems and some form of sectoral no-lose crediting. In order to reach this goal, major companies internationally—notably those in developing countries—have to participate and support a system with stringent targets and sanction mechanisms. The no-lose pledges in particular raise the risk that developing countries do not fully contribute to the global target. Hence, companies in developing countries have to be encouraged in meeting their targets through the adoption of adequate mechanisms (e.g., accelerated technology diffusion) and incentives (e.g., tradable permits). Furthermore, many industry representatives who support sectoral approaches suggest calculating the amount of greenhouse gases in terms of "carbon efficiencies" for the benchmarking system. These relative measurements are able to illustrate improvements per produced product or sales unit. However, in cases where consumption increases, emissions also increase. The global consequence may be that there is actually no real effect in terms of mitigating climate change.

If it is the intention to actually implement a sectoral approach that includes greenhouse gas reduction targets, all these limitations are important aspects that need to be addressed by climate policy experts. If this is not the case, sectoral approaches can nevertheless play an important role for the sharing of technology and knowledge, especially between companies in developed and developing countries. In sum, sectoral approaches offer a new focus for international climate negotiations. Instead of focusing on individual countries and their reduction targets, the focus is laid on specific carbon-intense industries on a global level. Based on existing initiatives (Busch *et al.* 2008), the money in the carbon-equal fund may be used to start further such initiatives and establish the monetary foundation and adequate incentives for technology and knowledge sharing.

## Fostering of low-carbon entrepreneurship

Our third suggestion for possible uses of the carbon-equal fund is to explicitly initiate new businesses targeting local climate change mitigation. Entrepreneurs, who require initial capital to get their business started, could benefit substantially from this financial aid. As such, we believe there is the need for a systematic funding of low-carbon entrepreneurship throughout the developing and developed world. Right now it seems that there are many excellent ideas on how we could actually curb greenhouse gas emissions, but we do not see a widespread realization of these ideas. In the following, we illustrate this in detail by referring to three examples, all taken from the same context of deforestation as this is a key area for international action (UNDP 2007) and a prime example of effective climate change mitigation that still faces serious issues in terms of its widespread implementation (Chatterjee 2009).

Curbing deforestation is a highly cost-effective way of reducing greenhouse gas emissions and their accumulation in the atmosphere because forests are a natural carbon sink (Stern 2006). Hence, reducing emissions from deforestation and forest degradation (REDD) and enhancing sustainable management of forests and forest carbon stocks (REDD+) are an important mitigation strategy. Deforestation accounts for about 18 percent of global greenhouse gas emissions, which is larger than the entire global transportation sector (Angelsen *et al.* 2009). The majority of the world's forests are located in developing nations. These countries are usually using forests as an economic resource. Therefore, measures should be financed by the developed world to protect the ecological services provided by forests. Research has found that afforestation projects in the tropics would be beneficial in terms of mitigating global warming; however, they would be counterproductive at high latitudes and offer only marginal benefits in temperate regions (Bala *et al.* 2007). As such the effectiveness of such projects depends on the location. Nevertheless, afforestation projects could serve as an important natural sink for carbon dioxide.

Initiating large-scale afforestation projects in suitable regions, however, poses certain problems. In many cases the interests of global companies, for example the palm oil industry, trigger the deforestation in developing countries. Although there are some efforts to stop activities in this regard, for example the Roundtable on Sustainable Palm Oil,[4] more efforts on the international policy level are required. The Kyoto Protocol, for example, did not include the management of forests and sinks on a comprehensive basis.

We believe that there is a huge opportunity for low-carbon entrepreneurship in the afforestation and reforestation context. With our first example, we refer to biologist Willie Smits who demonstrates that reforestation is a viable business model.[5] By regrowing a clearcut rainforest in Borneo he is able to actively develop a carbon sink and simultaneously solve a multitude of social problems and create jobs. Although this is only a small project with limited effects in terms of its climate change mitigation potential, it effectively demonstrates how reforestation can take place, how local climate can change, and how the negative effects of deforestation can be reversed. Based on the money from the carbon-equal fund, industrial policies for addressing climate change could take his experiences and develop mechanisms that provide the required start-up finances and ensure the profitability of such business models. This mainly would require setting incentives: on the one hand, for individuals to initiate similar projects; and on the other hand, for regions and communities in the developing world to create conditions such that these projects are as profitable as the alternative, which is to use the land in an unsustainable manner. Smits has shown that both objectives can be fulfilled: an active contribution to curbing climate change while improving economic welfare and social systems.

A very similar, but bigger in scope, example is the REDD Forests Tasmania Project, which is located in the state of Tasmania, Australia. The area is one of the most complex bioregions in Tasmania and has a large diversity of native vegetation. However, the region has a history of logging with drier forests. This project site historically was logged for pulpwood and firewood. The project improved forestry

4  www.rspo.org (accessed March 1, 2011).
5  www.ted.com/speakers/willie_smits.html (accessed March 1, 2011).

management and is designed to prove the commercial viability of using the carbon market to generate a viable alternative income for landowners to traditional logging income. Moreover, the project will protect native and old-growth forests for a 25-year period from deforestation and degradation. It is estimated that, by 2035, the project activities will have protected an old growth forest that, if cleared (i.e., without the project), would correspond to roughly 180,000 tons of carbon dioxide. Also, if replaced by a monoculture plantation of non-native exotic eucalypts still about 70,000 tons of greenhouse gas sequestration would be lost. Therefore the project will provide improved income-earning potential for the landowner and surrounding communities by substituting income from carbon sequestration for income from logging while abating carbon emissions. Based on these experiences with rather bigger projects, the carbon-equity fund could target getting similar projects off the ground in other regions of the world.

For our third example of low-carbon entrepreneurship we refer to the project management side. Similar to the Clean Development Mechanism and the related carbon market, reducing emissions from deforestation and forest degradation could also create an entire new finance and consultancy segment. It could fund projects that go beyond deforestation and forest degradation by including the role of conservation, sustainable management of forests, and enhancement of forest carbon stocks (REDD+). This new segment would be specialized in initiating forest projects and matching investors with regions in the developing world. The United Nations estimate that the financial flows for greenhouse gas emission reductions from such projects could reach up to $30 billion a year.[6] One very promising new project in this regard that has already been set up is the BaumInvest Reforestation Project, whose aims focus on ecological reforestation, intermediate cropping and reestablishing nature reserves.[7] Investors can expect a return on investment of approximately 6 percent per annum. Another example is the Madre de Dios Amazon Deforestation and Forest Degradation Project in Peru. The project has been

6  www.un-redd.org/AboutREDD/tabid/582/Default.aspx (accessed March 1, 2011).
7  www.bauminvest.de (accessed March 1, 2011).

approved according to the Climate, Community and Biodiversity Standards[8] and obtained the Gold Level as a result of its high social and environmental sustainability. In May 2010, the project was able to sell its first 40,000 tons of carbon dioxide at $7 per carbon certificate.[9] In general, the carbon-equal fund could facilitate the founding of further similar initiatives.

# The sequestration time bomb

Approaching the end of this chapter, we would like to reflect on two frequently discussed options for which we cannot see any need for financial support by a carbon-equal fund. In the context of global climate efforts, carbon sequestration—also referred to as carbon capture and storage (CCS)—is often discussed as a solution. For example, Socolow *et al.* (2004) discuss fifteen different technological solutions to stabilize climate change. They propose a number of wedge strategies, each one capable of avoiding one billion tons of carbon emissions per year by 2054. Beyond suggestions for wedges that aim to increase energy and carbon efficiencies and substitute fossil fuels by renewable energy sources, the authors suggest three stabilization wedges that include carbon capture and storage.

Carbon sequestration aims at capturing carbon dioxide from large sources such as fossil fuel power plants or carbon-dioxide-releasing chemical processes. The carbon dioxide would not be released into the atmosphere and instead it would be stored underground. Although this technology is still under development, the Swedish energy company Vattenfall, which started operating a 30 MW coal-based power plant alongside a carbon sequestration facility Schwarze Pumpe in Germany south of Berlin in September 2008, has showed its general feasibility in a pilot project. Despite its apparent feasibility, a clear disadvantage of this technology is its energy inefficiency. As discussed in a special report on carbon capture and storage by the Intergovernmental Panel on Climate Change (IPCC

8  www.climate-standards.org/projects/index.html (accessed March 1, 2011).
9  www.greenoxx.com/en/index.asp (accessed March 14, 2011).

2005), capturing and compressing carbon dioxide from a coal-fired power plant would require about 24–40 percent additional energy (fuel) in order to produce the same amount of electricity. At the same time, the power plant would not be carbon-free as current public debates suggest; the capture process would only reduce the amount of carbon dioxide emissions per kWh by 81–88 percent.

Proponents of this approach consider carbon sequestration as a vital option for addressing climate change and emphasize that it is especially important in light of the current developments in China, where nearly every week a new coal-fired power plant starts to generate energy. It is suggested that those power plants be equipped with post-combustion carbon capture and storage at a later stage, once the CCS technology becomes feasible. Irrespective of these facts, carbon sequestration cannot be regarded as an optimal solution for two reasons. First, it is only a temporary solution. Given that the carbon crisis also comprises the carbon input dimension, scarce and expensive fossil fuels will eventually make the utilization of renewable energy sources inevitable from a cost perspective. Second, the process of storing carbon dioxide under the surface is similar to sitting on a time bomb. There is the risk that, at some point, the storage facility will no longer be able to hold the stored carbon dioxide. Once it is released back to the surface, people living close to the leakage face a serious risk: carbon dioxide in high concentrations is a severe liability for every form of living organism. Although the specific risks are very different, there are certain parallels to the discussion of permanent disposal of nuclear waste. For example, a recent investigation revealed that the radioactive waste storage site at Asse in Germany released contaminated water; this was not captured in the report written by an expert who had previously attested this storage place to be secure. The same problem is relevant for carbon sequestration. There is no guarantee that the stored carbon dioxide will actually remain stored underground forever. Even though industrial policies for climate change mitigation may focus more on this as a potential solution, if there is no public acceptance and a belief in the technology, then there will be no large-scale implementation of it. As this solution bears a particularly high risk for future generations, we suggest that there should be no financial aid from a carbon-equal fund for developing and applying this technology further.

## The questionable solutions of geoengineering

Another example in this regard is geoengineering—also referred to as earth systems engineering—which has been an emerging topic in recent debates on addressing climate change. In September 2009 the UK Royal Society released a study investigating the geoengineering options that are available and concluded that engineering proposals to reduce the impact of climate change are "technically possible" (The Royal Society 2009). Professor John Shepherd, who chaired the Royal Society's geoengineering study, stressed that, even though it is essential for society to strive to cut emissions, we must also prepare for the possibility that this will fail and, therefore, have a "plan B" ready.

The Royal Society's study divides geoengineering methods into two basic types of technique. The first type is the carbon dioxide removal techniques, which remove carbon dioxide from the atmosphere. These target one of the main causes of climate change—rising carbon dioxide concentrations—and have relatively low uncertainties and risks associated with them. However, as a reduction of carbon dioxide emissions in the atmosphere requires decades to effectively contribute to cooling of the planet, these techniques work slowly and face similar problems to those discussed for carbon sequestration. In the second technique, referred to as solar radiation management, the sun's light and heat are reflected back into space. These methods target an increasing number of atmospheric reflecting particles in the stratosphere and thus represent an option to lower global temperatures quickly. As suggested by the study, if temperatures are to rise to such a level where more rapid action needs to be taken, the solar radiation management techniques were considered to have the most potential.

Solar radiation management techniques can be divided into three categories. First, atmospheric reflecting particles are used in the stratosphere to reflect parts of the incoming solar radiation. Several researchers consider such techniques as a feasible method as they imitate previous volcanic eruptions, which have been shown to effectively contribute to short-term temperature decreases. However, there are some serious questions over adverse effects, including the depletion of stratospheric ozone or ocean acidification. Second, space-based methods are discussed as a long-term solution by placing reflecting mirrors outside the Earth's atmosphere. Presently, these techniques are considered to be rather expensive, complex, difficult and slow to implement. Third, cloud albedo approaches involve ships in the ocean producing clouds, which would contribute to a drop in temperatures. However, the feasibility and effectiveness of this technique are not well understood. A great deal more research would be needed before this technique could be seriously considered.

Many proponents of geoengineering point out that this option would be more cost-effective compared with other adaptation and abatement costs and there would be immediate effects in terms of cooling the planet. As such, they consider geoengineering as one of the few solutions we have to prevent radical climate change. However the discussion above illustrates that the options suffer in two main respects. First, all of the solutions have to be regarded as end-of-pipe solutions. That is, they only temporarily solve the issue and some may even be considered as nothing more than a quick-and-dirty fix. The issue with these solutions is that the intensified accumulation of greenhouse gases in the atmosphere remains. Second, some of the technology is not yet formed and there are major uncertainties regarding its effectiveness, costs, and environmental impacts (The Royal Society 2009). Notably a reduction of incoming radiation might have substantial effects on regional precipitation. In a recent *Science* article Hegerl and Solomon (2009) conclude that geoengineering could lead to conflicts over water resources and may have the potential to lead to global migration and instability. In sum, the authors conclude that geoengineering bears an inappropriate risk to the health of our society and to the planet. Therefore, this option of addressing the global challenge of climate change is not very appealing. Instead, the risk of geoengineering resulting in an abrupt climate change "could be much higher than from unabated greenhouse gas emissions alone" (Gulledge 2008: 125). As a consequence, although many scientists currently call for additional research funds to investigate the feasibility of geoengineering, we suggest that a carbon-equal fund should focus on supporting efforts to effectively mitigate climate change, which target real and sustainable solutions instead of temporarily reducing the inconvenient outcome.

# 10

# Meso level
## Inter-firm breakthrough steps in a low-carbon future

Identifying the underlying problem is quite straightforward when looking at the sources of a potential global carbon crisis from an industrial ecology point of view (for general introductions see Ayres and Ayres 2002; Graedel and Allenby 2003). In ecological systems the natural loops between individual system components are closed. This means that the output of one system's component is used as an input for another system's component. In the carbon context, the most suitable example is natural photosynthesis. Based on this idea of closing loops of material flows, industrial ecology scientists argue that single firms on their own often have a limited capacity for reducing their carbon throughput. In other words, firms operating individually are less efficient and have a larger carbon footprint. Instead, inter-firm collaboration, referred to as the "industrial ecosystem," holds great potential through knowledge sharing, development of mutual assets, and sharing of costs: for example, for research and development expenses and infrastructure investments. These more conceptual considerations are supported by the following empirical examples.

# Industrial symbiosis in the carbon context

Companies have a major role to play in attempting to achieve a low-carbon society. In recent years a number of initiatives have been developed in the direction of industrial symbiosis, which also contribute to increased carbon efficiencies. Operating on the premise that waste products from some companies might be useful materials to others, many material exchange networks have been developed across the world in order to enable businesses to find either a market or an end user for something that they cannot use themselves. Such exchange networks can be considered to be the most straightforward option of an industrial symbiosis approach. Online databases such as the US-based Recycler's World[1] allow businesses to add listings or to search for specific resources, thus facilitating the trading of scrap and waste materials. These networks therefore promote collaboration and foster mutually beneficial relationships between companies to ensure the optimization of resource use, collecting information, and acting as a facilitator through which companies can interact. This is extremely positive from a climate perspective as the extraction and production of materials is accompanied by carbon emissions, and therefore the reuse of existing materials results in significant carbon emission reductions. The Chicago Waste to Profit Network, for example, managed to reduce carbon emissions by 50,000 tons by the end of its pilot year (Mangan and Olivetti 2008).

Participating within such networks is not entirely altruistic behavior on the part of companies. It can be socially and economically advantageous. The cooperation and environmental benefits created can result in greatly improved perceptions of a company among consumers and the local community, improved reputation, political goodwill, and can enhance a company's networking opportunities (Mangan and Olivetti 2008). Furthermore, potential improvements in efficiency and productivity may be realized, along with material diversion from landfills and savings that come from avoiding disposal and transportation costs. As such, these networks provide

---

1  www.recycle.net (accessed March 1, 2011).

companies with the opportunity to turn a previously useless waste product into something that generates additional revenue.

Some companies even took a step further by creating a tighter and longer-term exchange system. In such cases, companies establish a mutually beneficial collaboration, which enables them to commercially utilize each other's residual and by-products, resulting in reduced environmental impact through the reduction of both waste and energy used in creating new products. One of the most prominent examples is the industrial symbiosis network in Kalundborg, Denmark.[2] It has several key members from different industries: a Statoil oil refinery, Novo Nordisk pharmaceutical plant, enzyme producer Novozymes, Dong Energy's Asnæs power station, plasterboard producer Gyproc A/S, soil remediation company RGS 90 A/S, Kara/Noveren waste company, and Kalundborg Municipality (see Fig. 11). The overall goal of this network is to improve efficiency and promote development, the exchange of information, and the utilization of by-products to reduce the use of resources. At present, this collaboration consists of over twenty projects with the purpose of reusing or creating new resources, and finding means of utilizing by-products, which may initially seem to have no feasible use or value. Again, this reuse of resources means that the emission-intensive initial extraction and production of materials is avoided. For example, energy reductions have been achieved through the use of the excess heat generated during the production of electricity at Asnæs power station to provide process steam to the Statoil A/S oil refinery, Novo Nordisk A/S, Novozymes A/S, and central heating to Kalundborg.

Similarly, there is a financial incentive for the members of the symbiosis network in Kalundborg to undertake such activities. This incentive may not only be associated with the value of the material that is being exchanged; instead, it is generated by indirect upstream or downstream economic effects. Indeed, in some cases the direct economic benefits may be minimal and exchanges will often be prompted by longer-term strategic considerations regarding production, security of supply, operational capabilities, and so forth (Jacobsen 2006). Examples such as Kalundborg illustrate new ways in which businesses can reduce their environmental impact. Yet most

2 www.symbiosis.dk (accessed March 1, 2011).

Figure 11 **Industrial symbiosis network in Kalundborg**

Source: www.symbiosis.dk

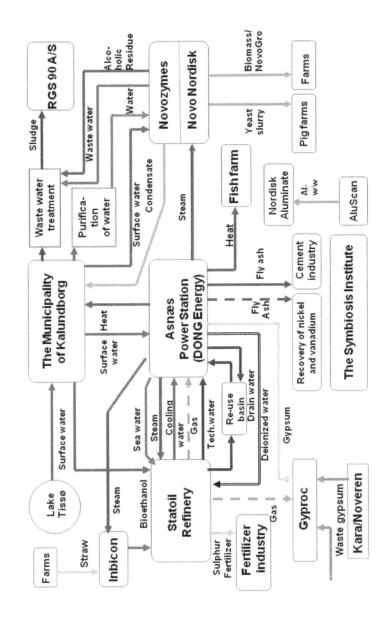

industrial symbioses are not explicitly focused on climate change and carbon reductions. Given that businesses have a substantial contribution to the evolving carbon crisis and firms will be increasingly exposed to carbon constraints, it is important that they incorporate low-carbon thinking within their overall strategies. The collaborations described here therefore may serve as valuable blueprints for further developments towards a climate friendly economy. The following two examples illustrate this by "challenging the desert."

## DESERTEC: Challenging the desert I

Efforts to establish an industrial symbiosis-oriented production system can encourage collaborations between companies and expand over entire cities or regions. For example, Babcock Ranch is an ambitious city development project in Florida, which was purchased in a unique deal between the state and federal governments, environmentalist groups, and a property developer.[3] The intention is to develop a climate-friendly city based on solar power. The most prominent example in this context is the DESERTEC project, which is hailed by some as being the most ambitious and large-scale project conceived in renewable energy to date. Founded by the Trans-Mediterranean Renewable Energy Cooperation (TREC) network, the project aims to provide carbon-free energy to Europe, North Africa, and the Middle East using renewable energy technologies. DESERTEC's vision is to assist in overcoming the current barriers to renewable energy, by combining the resources of Europe, the Middle East, and North Africa so that each of these respective regions are in a much better position to shift to clean and secure energy rapidly and economically (DESERTEC Foundation 2009).

A key aspect of the DESERTEC concept is harvesting solar energy from North African deserts based on concentrating solar power plants. These plants would be supplemented by other means of renewable energy generation such as wind, hydro, biomass, or geothermal sources across Europe. Each of these reflects the local

3 www.babcockranchflorida.com (accessed March 1, 2011).

conditions in the different areas: for example, offshore wind energy would be produced in the UK or geothermal power in Italy, and then exported to the main centers of energy demand. As the current electricity networks are not built to transmit large amounts of electricity over such long distances, the installation of a large new electricity network using so-called "high-voltage direct current" transmission lines would be necessary to connect Europe, the Middle East, and North Africa.

Derived from an extensive analysis carried out by the German Aerospace Center (2005), the basic driver behind the project can be found on the DESERTEC web page: in general, within six hours deserts receive more energy from the sun than humankind consumes within a year.[4] Put differently, 1 percent of the area of global deserts would be sufficient to produce the entire annual global primary energy demand. This roughly corresponds to an area as big as Switzerland (see Fig. 12). For this reason, the project's focus is on solar

Figure 12 **Areas (white squares) required for concentrating solar power plants to generate as much electricity as is currently consumed by the world, the EU, and the Middle East and North Africa Region**

Source: DESERTEC Foundation 2009

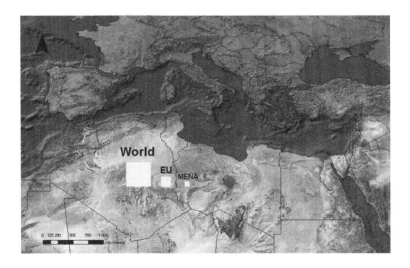

4 www.desertec.org (accessed March 1, 2011).

power generation: in comparison with other renewable energy technologies, the project initiators state that concentrating solar power bears the highest potential in terms of meeting global and expanding energy demand, and is theoretically fairly simple to harness.

Concentrating solar power plants require steam-generated power stations that produce heat from solar radiation harvested by solar collectors such as trough-shaped parabolic mirrors. These mirrors beam the concentrated radiation directly onto a tower receiver, which contains a heat transfer fluid, generally oil, and this fluid then passes through a "solar superheater." The heat is subsequently used to generate steam to drive the turbines of the generator which produces electricity that can be fed into the electricity transmission grid. The steam is later cooled using water from a cooling tower, and is fed back into the steam generator (for illustration see Fig. 13).

Besides providing a large area with carbon-free energy, the DESERTEC project may offer other benefits. One idea that is currently under investigation is the possibility of using seawater to cool the steam being produced which can be condensed and desalinized to make freshwater as a by-product of the generation process. This, combined with the shadow provided by the parabolic mirrors, may potentially be very useful for agricultural purposes in the arid, desert regions where the concentrating solar power plants are to be located. Furthermore, the thermo oil allows for short-term storage, and further storage can be realized through the use of molten salts. A decline in energy production on cloudy days, for example, can be supplemented by such storing efforts, or alternatively substituted with other production means such as biofuels when necessary. This is helpful not only to deal with fluctuations of solar radiation, but also in terms of providing flexibility to respond to temporarily changing energy demands. Finally, concentrating solar power technology and the required direct current transmission lines have the advantage of being a proven technology with several concentrating solar power plants already operating successfully around the globe. The first solar power generation plant was constructed by the US engineer Frank Shuman in Egypt in 1913. Another more recent example is the plant at Kramer Junction in California, which became operational in 1985. Companies such as Siemens who are actively involved

Figure 13 **Concentrating solar power generation**

Source: Quaschning 2010

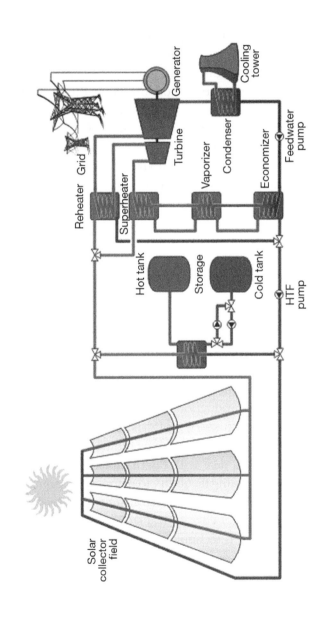

in the project development stage are utilizing the high-voltage direct current transmitting technology.

In spite of its apparent benefits, the DESERTEC project is not without its critics. Some point out that it will cost billions of dollars to build and transfer energy across long distances and thus the question arises whether such an initiative makes economic sense when renewable energy can be produced locally. Going beyond this, building solar power plants in politically unstable countries is deemed to be risky as it creates the same dependencies and uncertainties as those currently experienced by industrialized countries with respect to crude oil from the Middle East. The DESERTEC project, however, may go some way towards improving stability in these regions by offering economic benefits to the host countries in terms of creating jobs and infrastructure. On a similar note, the risk of terrorist attacks which could potentially cut off the energy supply is reduced by the project given that it is intended to use a wide range of locations and facilities and different transmission lines, thereby reducing the impact of a single devastating attack.

At the current stage, it is estimated that the project will cost €400 billion, the financing and further development of which is currently being pursued by dozens of finance and industrial firms mainly from Germany, which include Munich Re, Siemens, Deutsche Bank, and E.ON. Owing to the challenges ahead, one single company would have a hard time getting a project of this scope of the ground. Through this inter-firm collaboration—in a certain sense a large-scale industrial symbiosis project—all firms will benefit from a successful project. Although the project is still in its initial planning stages, it is believed that, once it becomes operational, DESERTEC could provide 15 percent of Europe's energy needs (Zeller 2009). At present, the project is focused on beginning negotiations for the implementation of the DESERTEC concept between Europe, North Africa, and the Middle East, campaigning to raise awareness of the project in these regions, establishing feasibility studies and pilot projects, and developing industrial capacity for solar thermal power plant construction.

# Masdar: Challenging the desert II

The Masdar Initiative was launched by the Government of the Emirate of Abu Dhabi in 2006 with the purpose of positioning Abu Dhabi as a global leader in renewable energies and sustainability. Its economy has been reliant on crude oil and gas exports from which it generates almost 70 percent of its total GDP (Reiche 2009). The finite nature of these resources coupled with Abu Dhabi's heavy reliance on such resources makes future economic diversification of paramount importance for this country. Rising energy demand and the threat of anthropogenic climate change, not to mention the relative abundance of energy received by Abu Dhabi in the form of solar radiation, makes renewable energy seem a logical choice for this region.

Masdar can be seen as a large-scale project inspired by the industrial symbiosis idea, transferring its basic premise to the vision of a low-carbon (or even carbon-neutral) city. One key factor is the close collaboration of different firms and agencies. Mandated to drive the Masdar Initiative is the Abu Dhabi Future Energy Company, which currently invests in various stages of this initiative ranging from research and development to commercial operations. In addition to this, the company acts as a project developer, embarks on joint ventures, and acquires innovative companies focusing on future technologies (Nader 2009). Masdar can therefore be broken down into five separate units. First, the Carbon Management Unit is in charge of the creation and management of greenhouse gas reduction projects under the provision of the Clean Development Mechanism framework of the Kyoto Protocol. Second, a $250 million venture capital clean-tech fund was launched in partnership with Credit Suisse, the Consensus Business Group, and Siemens in 2006. Masdar's Utilities and Asset Management Unit manages this. The third unit is Masdar's Industries Unit, which is responsible for the creation of Masdar's portfolio of production assets of which a key component is Masdar PV, a company that will manufacture thin-film photovoltaic modules. The fourth is Masdar Institute of Science and Technology, which was set up as a postgraduate educational and research facility, cooperating with the Massachusetts Institute of Technology (MIT) in Boston.

Perhaps most important, and certainly most newsworthy, is Masdar's fifth unit, the Property Development Unit, which has been assigned the task of constructing the world's largest carbon-neutral development to date, Masdar City (see Fig. 14). Construction of Masdar City began in 2008 and is scheduled for completion by 2016 at a cost of over $24 billion (Nader 2009). It is expected to cover an area of over 6 km$^2$ and will have a population of 40,000, with another 50,000 commuting into the city to work at some of the 15,000 companies it hopes to attract (Reiche 2009). In order to draw companies, particularly those in the field of sustainable energy, to the area, the Abu Dhabi government has made Masdar City a free zone, meaning that resident companies will benefit from zero taxes and zero import tariffs. One such organization that is to be located in Masdar City is the International Renewable Energy Agency (IRENA). Perhaps being attracted to the area by the promise of free office space, donations of $135 million to assist in its start-up phase, and $50 million to fund its various international projects, IRENA has announced Masdar City will host its secretariat.

Masdar City will utilize both traditional Arabic architecture and new renewable technologies. With its low-rise, high-density neighborhoods and its northeast/southwest orientation, Masdar City's architecture reduces solar glare and maximizes the cooling winds coming from the gulf and the desert thereby limiting the energy used in cooling systems. Designed by the London architects Foster & Partners, Masdar City aims to use 100 percent renewable energy, produce zero waste through a process of reducing, reusing, recycling, and energy capture, and to be a center of excellence in the field of sustainable technology. Water will also be recycled and transportation within the city limited to specially designed light rail and personal rapid transport systems.

Masdar City will run on a combination of renewable energies, an obvious one of which, given its location, is solar. The two methods of capturing solar energy currently planned for Masdar City are photovoltaic and concentrating solar power. Photovoltaic cells are made of silicon semiconductors and produce direct current electricity from the sunlight. Concentrating solar power plants, meanwhile, produce heat from solar radiation, which is collected by parabolic mirrors

Figure 14 **Artist's impression highlighting the proposed master plan of Masdar City**

Source: courtesy of Masdar City

(see also the DESERTEC example). The use of wind turbines to generate energy from desert winds is also under discussion. In addition, geothermal power, which is the extraction of energy from heat stored in the earth, may be obtained from a system of ground-source heat pumps and high-density polyethylene pipes, which contain a heat transfer fluid. In order to maximize resource utilization, desalinization of water through reverse osmosis is planned.

Masdar City is a very ambitious project and it still remains uncertain whether the targets set will be met in terms of the environmental objectives as well as in terms of the number of residents and companies it seeks to attract. Nevertheless, the Masdar Initiative is an exciting project, which explores the possibilities offered by renewable energy and the industrial symbiosis idea in a community context. Unprecedented in scale, Masdar City has huge potential: the ideas of closed loops and the focus on sustainable technologies could potentially act as a blueprint for other regions and spur policies for new low-carbon collaborations between firms elsewhere.

# 11
# Micro level
## Proactive carbon management strategies

In Chapter 10 we discussed examples of inter-firm collaboration and cooperation as options for fostering the industrial path towards a low-carbon society. In order to reap the rewards of increased carbon efficiencies—which not only exist between firms but can also be found within companies—proactive carbon management is required. There are several motivations for companies to choose to engage in curbing their emissions and reducing their carbon dependence. Rooted in their ecological responsibility (Bansal and Roth 2000), many companies may do so because management is simply convinced that this is the right way to run a company in the 21st century. We highly value such efforts and believe that such an understanding is essential for any well-managed company. However, Chicago School-inspired managers and business students may ask whether carbon management actually pays off. As such, we take a clear instrumental perspective with this micro-level chapter and seek to demonstrate that there is a business case for corporate carbon management.

In the management literature, several authors have discussed how firms can establish competitive advantage by mindfully moving towards climate-friendly structures (e.g., Schultz and Williamson

2005; Porter and Reinhardt 2007). Depending on the industry, the most effective carbon reductions may be realized within upstream (suppliers) or downstream (customers) processes, or firm-internally. It is therefore important to first consider the whole value chain as the scope for potential carbon management actions and then decide—depending on the magnitude of the identified carbon reduction potential—which specific aspects within the value chain should be targeted for optimizations.

Based on this scope, management can focus on different target areas for implementing a carbon management strategy. We elaborate on those, referring to the previously introduced (see Chapter 2) vision, inputs, throughputs, and outputs (VITO) elements of an environmental management strategy (Shrivastava 1995c). **Inputs** refer to energy conservation, materials recycling, and the reduction of virgin and hazardous materials. In the carbon management context, the strategy can seek to substitute carbon-containing materials. Furthermore, carbon reductions within the supply chain can be targeted (e.g., Kolk and Pinkse 2005). For example, for a metal-processing firm the upstream processes are usually the most relevant in terms of their carbon reduction potential. **Throughputs**, meanwhile, refer to improvements in production efficiency and pollution prevention. With regard to carbon management, internal carbon optimizations can be achieved through more efficient use of fossil fuels (e.g., Hoffman 2006). For a cement production company, for instance, the firm-internal processes are particularly significant for carbon optimizations as the calcination process causes the majority of carbon dioxide emissions. **Outputs** refer to environmentally sound product designs or packaging. Here, the carbon efficiency of products and services during their usage phase can be enhanced (e.g., Okereke 2007). This is most relevant in industries with products and services that are carbon-intensive during the usage phase, such as in the automotive sector. The fourth element, **vision**, reflects the overall understanding and implementation of environmental responsibilities. In the carbon management context, it is important to establish and communicate a clear commitment towards a low-carbon future. Within this commitment companies can—beyond the efforts described above—seek to become carbon-neutral and offset emissions that cannot be reduced through their own efforts. Based on these identified elements three main drivers may contribute to maintaining and enhancing competitiveness in the carbon management context: cost reductions, enhanced legitimacy, and revenue increase (see Fig. 15).

Figure 15 **Drivers of corporate carbon management**

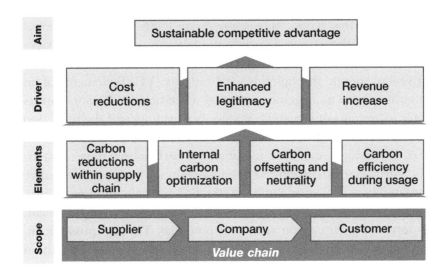

## Cost reductions

Corporate carbon management can seek to increase productivity and reduce operational costs (Porter and Reinhardt 2007). This idea goes back to Porter's (1980) industrial organization view in which an important source of competitiveness at the industrial level arises from achieving lower costs than rivals. Such cost improvements can be realized either through process innovations, which are accompanied by savings of raw materials and other resources, or product-related changes, which for example result in lower packaging costs (Shrivastava 1995b). Our discussion about carbon constraints has illustrated that both process innovations and product-related changes have to be considered from a carbon input and output dimension in the context of carbon-related costs. In the input dimension, energy prices have been found to be important drivers related to carbon management (Jeswani *et al*. 2008; Okereke 2007). Companies seek to reduce energy costs because they are often the largest annual recurrent expenditure (Hoffman 2005). In the output dimension, the release of carbon dioxide constitutes an additional cost factor in countries that have established an emissions trading scheme. To illustrate, under the previously discussed European Union Emissions Trading Scheme companies must purchase additional allowances should their emission level be above the allowances they have been allocated. An alternative option, however, is to internally increase carbon efficiency and save those costs. On the national level an increasing number of mandatory carbon trading schemes are in discussion or are scheduled to be enacted in the next few years (see Chapter 9). For example, New Zealand has passed regulations with concrete time plans.

Once implemented, regulations pertaining to the carbon input and/or output impact the majority of companies within an economy (Kolk and Hoffmann 2007). Even though certain carbon regulations are not yet enforced, proactive carbon strategies are a matter of fiduciary obligation and guide against risk (Okereke 2007). As a result, for most businesses, reducing energy and fossil fuel consumption is important from a current and future cost perspective. Notably, many carbon improvements are possible without any significant investments and are accompanied by immediate benefits in terms of cost savings. These "low-hanging fruits" can easily be realized. For example, Walmart has a fleet of over 50,000 trucks. All these trucks were leaving the main engine running to keep the driver's cabin warm/cool when the truck was not moving (eight hours per night). The company realized that a 500 horsepower engine was not necessary to drive a small cabin heater/cooler and that an auxiliary engine could be used as a substitute. Although in the long run the company will need to redesign its transportation and delivery strategy because of emerging carbon constraints, in the short run the little step described above allowed the company to save thousands of dollars and tons in fossil fuel, and carbon emissions. Moreover, it is important that firms take into account the entire value chain in light of emerging carbon constraints: effective carbon management can enhance competitiveness within upstream, downstream, and firm-internal processes. For example, the UK retailer Marks & Spencer has reduced the carbon footprint of its food products by focusing on its supply chain and by sourcing seasonal goods locally. In addition, the firm has supported the development of more energy-efficient textile factories in the UK, China, and Sri Lanka under the umbrella of "Plan A," which has set the goal for M&S to become the world's most sustainable retailer.[1]

# Enhanced legitimacy

When analyzing the motivations for corporate environmental responsiveness, legitimacy is also an important driver (Bansal and Roth 2000). Literature on institutional theory argues that success and competitiveness is affected by the degree to which firms conform to expectations and demands in their institutional environment (Meyer and Rowan 1977; Oliver 1991; Powell and DiMaggio 1991; Scott 2001). Over time, organizations seek to adapt their structures, practices, and resource investments in order to gain, maintain, or repair legitimacy, which can be defined as the generalized perception that the actions of a firm are desirable, proper, or appropriate (Suchman 1995). As gaining legitimacy has been found to be a necessary precondition for firms to generate a good corporate reputation (Doh *et al.* 2010), there is a direct link to competitiveness.

The relevance of legitimacy-enhancing activities in the context of climate change can be derived from Hoffman's (1999) notion that organizational fields form around central issues. An organizational field is defined as "those organizations that, in aggregate, constitute a recognized area of institutional life: key suppliers, resource and product consumers, regulatory agencies, and other organizations that produce similar services or products" (DiMaggio and Powell 1983: 148). In the carbon management context—beyond the central role of governments—important organizations are NGOs, suppliers,

---

1 See plana.marksandspencer.com (accessed March 14, 2011).

competitors, investors, consumers, and employees (Kolk and Pinkse 2007). This group of actors composes a firm's organizational field in the context of climate change and their influence is manifested in specific rules, norms, and beliefs with respect to a firm's carbon management practices. For example, employees may prefer working for an employer that actively addresses climate change (Hoffman 2005). With respect to the value chain, new pressures have also recently emerged. A case in point is the US retailer Walmart, which has developed a sustainability index intended to move its suppliers and retail competitors towards more sustainable business practices.[2] As a core component of the questionnaire the suppliers are asked for their levels of greenhouse gas emissions, corresponding reduction targets, and energy costs. Furthermore, actors on financial markets have increasingly requested companies to disclose information concerning their carbon footprints, reduction measures, and climate-change-related risks (Hoffman 2006; Okereke 2007; Jeswani *et al.* 2008). Examples are the Carbon Disclosure Project, the Investors Group on Climate Change, and Ceres. As such, climate change has to be regarded as a central issue that forms an organizational field and companies are able to achieve a high level of legitimacy through whole-life-cycle carbon management, which in turn maintains and enhances competitiveness compared with companies that fail to do so.

## Revenue increase

Several studies have shown that new market segments are emerging from growing consumer concerns about the natural environment (Roberts 1996; Trudel and Cotte 2009; Zimmer *et al.* 1994). Thus, options to increase competitive advantage arise from the ability to offer new or improved products that justify a premium price and thus generate additional revenues (Porter 1980). As such, proactive companies are able to achieve market differentiation by pursuing a

2 See www.pressreleasepoint.com/walmart-index-tout-ecofriendly-products (accessed March 1, 2011).

low-carbon branding strategy and increase revenues among environmentally sensitive customers (Hart 1995; Russo and Fouts 1997).

Especially in the climate change context, companies face a market transition towards "new competitive environments where some will decline, while others rise to fill their place" (Hoffman 2005: 22-23). This transition creates demand for new low-carbon innovations, which generate new options for corporate differentiation through better products and services:

> Some firms, in the process of addressing climate change, will find opportunities to enhance or extend their competitive positioning by creating products (such as hybrid cars) that exploit climate-induced demand, by leading the restructuring of their industries to address climate issues more effectively, or by innovating in activities affected by climate change to produce a genuine competitive advantage (Porter and Reinhardt 2007: 22).

For example, cumulative installed photovoltaic capacity has increased more than tenfold between 2000 and 2008 (EPIA 2009). Although the industry has been hit hard by the economic downturn, cumulative installed capacity is expected to increase by 13–20 percent per annum over the coming years (EPIA 2009). In the long term, the growth prospects of the industry are very positive given that photovoltaic electricity could become fully cost-competitive around 2020 (Bagnall and Boreland 2008). As such, companies are able to generate a competitive advantage through carbon management efforts that target the development and production of low-emission products and services. In sum, proactive carbon management strategies can manifest in two basic directions: reengineering for a carbon-efficient organization and exploration of new low-carbon business opportunities.

# Reengineering for a carbon-efficient organization

In order to get started on becoming a carbon-efficient organization we introduce an easy-to-handle-and-establish corporate carbon management framework, which was developed and applied within a two-year pilot project at the Swiss Federal Institute of Technology by Holger Hendrichs, who successfully consults companies on related topics. This framework is based on seven steps, which are illustrated in Figure 16. We discuss each step and reflect on experiences from applying the framework in several empirical case studies.

Figure 16 **Corporate carbon management framework**

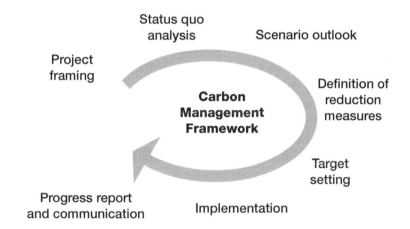

## Project framing

In step one, the general project needs to be framed. Important aspects need to be discussed and agreed upon: for example, which company activities shall be covered (complete company, single processes, single products), which greenhouse gas emissions scopes (WBCSD and WRI 2004) shall be covered, and whether the focus is on carbon inputs, outputs, or both. Furthermore, it is important to develop a formal project structure, determine who is internally responsible for managing the project, and lay the internal foundations for a systematic carbon information management system. Our case studies illustrated that it is also helpful to compile an overview over already existing activities focusing on climate mitigation or energy issues, which in almost every firm exist at least to a certain minimum. Moreover, such activities are often simply not explicitly labeled or considered as "carbon management improvements." An overview of such activities provides a good summary of the current carbon management efforts and leads to a positive attitude towards the project: employees realize that they do not have to start from scratch and that improvements are actually feasible. Usually initial ideas for carbon management improvements can already be gathered within this first step.

## Status quo analysis

In step two, data is collected to calculate a company's current (status quo) carbon performance for the chosen project focus. Usually managers and employees refer to this step as the "$CO_2$ footprint" or "carbon footprint" calculation. The most important methodic guideline for the required carbon accounting is the "Greenhouse Gas Protocol" jointly released by the World Business Council for Sustainable Development and World Resources Institute (WBCSD and WRI 2004). The protocol differentiates between three greenhouse gas emission scopes: emissions stemming from own combustion processes (Scope 1); indirect emissions caused by the production of externally purchased energy (Scope 2); and further indirect emissions relating to upstream and downstream process steps (Scope 3). For a comprehensive analysis of emission reduction opportunities (see step four) it is important that firms know their most important emission sources. Thus, the complete value chain including the products and services usage phase with consumers should be reflected on. In many of our case studies the inclusion of Scope 3 emissions was essential for identifying the most effective reduction opportunities. However, assessing scope 3 emissions in detail is still difficult (Busch 2010). Based on the resulting information about the firm's carbon flows, two important corporate carbon performance indicators can be determined: carbon intensity and carbon exposure (see Glossary). Based on the resulting snapshot of the firm's carbon performance, the success in carbon improvements can be evaluated at a later stage.

## Scenario outlook

In step three, a scenario outlook is conducted, which analyzes corporate sensitivity towards carbon-related changes in the business environment. This step requires the definition of carbon scenarios, which need to consider market forecasts for carbon prices, carbon in- and output patterns of the analyzed industry, and further company-specific aspects. Such scenarios should incorporate developments regarding fossil fuel consumption (for example, the oil consumption in future years) and estimate the potential additional costs (for example, the price increases for energy and possible carbon taxes). Based on this, possible financial implications of the current carbon and energy utilization and emissions taxes become transparent. Our cases illustrated that many companies were not aware of the magnitude of these potential costs. Beyond this, depending on the industrial sector and the product portfolio, firms may also extend the scenarios by possible customer and marketing trends. Based on the information obtained through this scenario outlook, the expected future carbon performance can be anticipated and potential "carbon risks" become visible (see Glossary).

## Definition of reduction measures

In step four, a comparative analysis has to reveal which reduction measures will be targeted. Some reduction measures may be obvious (low-hanging fruits) while others require significant investments and have a rather long-term payback. In order to find and assess adequate options for greenhouse gas emissions reductions through technological or organizational optimizations, detailed knowledge about the company's production processes and organizational procedures is required. Moreover, we highlighted above that a whole-value-chain perspective on greenhouse gas emission levels is essential for significant system-wide greenhouse gas reductions. As such, emission reduction measures can generally focus on three levels: company-internal processes (Scope 1 emissions, Scope 2 emissions when the energy use is considered); the optimization of pre-products from suppliers (Scope 3 emissions); or the utilization phase of end-products (Scope 3 emissions). Experiences showed that corporate management and the designated project manager usually lack specific information about individual options for emission reductions. Throughout the case studies we could confirm the not very surprising circumstance that employees working in a specific area typically know best about their daily routines and tasks and thus they are well positioned to identify technological or organizational optimization options for achieving emissions reductions. Furthermore, the efforts discussed above for knowledge transfer, for example through local climate agencies and sectoral approaches, could be another valuable information source in this context.

## Target setting

In step five, specific targets are set that reflect the reduction potentials of the previously defined measures. There are generally three options for setting a target: first, an absolute target expressed as the percentage of total emissions compared with a baseline year; second, a relative target based on an improvement of the firm's carbon intensity over a given time frame (e.g., total emissions over sales); and, third, a qualitative target describing the intended reduction measures and timeline for implementation. Corresponding targets serve as a guideline for the implementation of the measures and help to evaluate the success of their implementation. Furthermore, they may also serve as a means to demonstrate external commitment (see step seven). In this context, firms may consider offsetting certain emissions, which they themselves are unable to reduce. However, this should be the last option, as for effective system-wide reductions, all potentials need to be reaped. The main focus is on setting realistic targets and seeking to meet those targets by their own efforts.

## Implementation

In step six the measures decided on in step four are implemented. For this step it is essential to break down the targets of step five at the business unit or product level. Next, employees are nominated to coordinate and control the implementation of individual measures step by step. Furthermore, our case studies illustrated the usefulness of defining timely and realistic intermediate steps and goals within the implementation process of individual measures, especially as, for many employees, carbon management is a new challenge that goes along with additional tasks. Such steps and goals help remind everyone about the project and allow for early corrections in case someone misses a deadline. Experiences also showed that it is crucial that the CEO or the company's owner gives top priority to the implementation measures and that he or she actively supports the entire project.

## Progress report and communication

In the last step, the company can use the results for reporting purposes. The objective of this step is to inform and interact with a company's stakeholders and to generate a high level of transparency with respect to the company's responses to climate change. In order to evaluate the progress being made, two indicators are helpful, carbon dependency and carbon risk. A firm's carbon dependency allows the assessment of the extent to which a firm's physical carbon performance has changed over time. A firm's carbon risk allows the assessment of the extent to which the financial implications of a firm's carbon usage have changed over time (see Glossary). Various stakeholders can be addressed by communicating the relevant messages. For suppliers, companies could elaborate on how emission reduction measures have led to an improvement across the whole supply chain. Progress achieved as well as new targets set can be used for informing investors: for example, via responses to the Carbon Disclosure Project. Within marketing, companies may seek to establish a low-carbon leadership position and attain socially conscious consumers with pro-climate attitudes. Internally, the successes of carbon management efforts can be highlighted and employees can be thanked for their cooperation and encouraged to further contribute to establishing a successful carbon management system. Beyond these voluntary communication efforts, companies increasingly face mandatory reporting guidelines, especially in the carbon risk context. For example, in February 2010 the US Securities and Exchange

Commission (SEC) released its guidance on disclosure related to business or legal developments regarding climate change.[3] This guidance mentions specific areas relevant for disclosure, if they constitute a material risk for a company. They include, existing and pending US climate-change-related laws and regulations; international accords and treaties relating to climate change; indirect consequence of regulations or business trends such as a decreased demand for goods that produce significant greenhouse gas emissions; and potential physical impacts of climate change such as damages to property. Based on the carbon management framework described, companies obtain information about their carbon risks which can be reported in response to the new disclosure rules.

# Exploration of new low-carbon business opportunities

There are many ways in which individual companies may explore new low-carbon business opportunities (Orsato 2006). In general, such an exploration can be achieved by focusing on one of the following two directions: develop a new product or service and enter an entire new market segment; or rethink and redesign the existing product and service portfolio. With respect to the former, the success of such a strategy depends on several factors such as the consumption patterns and the competitiveness structure of the new market segment. Regarding the latter, managers should step back and consider what the value, utility, or features is they provide to customers. In many cases it can be very important to dismiss the product focus for a moment and determine the actual demanded service. The example of "Better Place" illustrates such a service focus in two ways: it focuses on the provided service "miles driven by car" and offers a viable substitute for combustion engines; and it acknowledges the special service requirements of its customers and offers intelligent solutions.

3 www.sec.gov/news/press/2010/2010-15.htm (accessed March 2, 2011).

Better Place is an electric vehicle service provider with offices around the globe, headquartered in Palo Alto, California.[4] When the company was launched in 2007 electric vehicles faced several problems: they have consistently struggled to compete with their petrol-fueled counterparts in terms of cost and convenience; a key hindrance to the uptake of the electric vehicle is the battery necessary to power it. Batteries offering the same mileage and propulsion as a tank of fuel are cumbersome and costly, thus making an electric vehicle an expensive purchase and incapable of competing with the cheaper combustion engine. Furthermore, charging the battery itself can be inconvenient for the user as it is a lengthy process and it is also necessary to find an appropriate location to plug the car into the grid. Given that it is likely that most electric vehicle owners will charge their vehicles at the end of the day, there is also the possibility that the electricity grid could become overloaded.

To enable electric vehicles to compete with conventional oil-fueled automobiles, it is first necessary to lower the cost considerably for the customer. Better Place hopes to achieve this through the separation of the cost of the battery from the overall cost of the vehicle. This means that, rather than having to purchase the battery with the car, the customer leases the battery from Better Place at a monthly rate, which also covers the cost of recharging or swapping the battery when necessary. In addition, responsibility for battery maintenance is shifted from the consumer to the company itself and this further reduces the consumer's costs. The company currently offers a recyclable lithium-ion battery expected to last for up to eight years and capable of travelling 100 miles on a single charge, and is currently working with specialized battery manufacturers to develop more efficient batteries for future use.

The present inconveniences associated with charging are to be tackled through the installation of an extensive network of charge spots near homes, workplaces, and shopping centers and the building of switch stations, which automatically replace depleted batteries with fully charged ones within the space of a few minutes. A prototype of a battery switch station was demonstrated in Japan at the end of 2009 and involves the car releasing its battery onto a platform raised by

4  www.betterplace.com (accessed March 2, 2011).

hydraulics and then picking up another fully charged battery from a second platform. This process takes less than two minutes. Electric vehicles themselves will be equipped with software which tracks battery levels and directs the driver towards the nearest charge spot or switch station before the battery runs out. Additionally, Better Place hopes to overcome the issue of limits to grid capacity through the introduction of a demand management system whereby the distribution of electricity to each car can be monitored and managed rather than the vehicle simply being charged automatically the moment it is plugged in (Bullis 2008). As a result, the traditional problems associated with certain forms of renewable energy—namely, unpredictability of supply and intermittency—would not be an issue. Indeed, wind energy is a good match for electric vehicles as they are typically recharged at night when wind turbines generate electricity and demand for energy is otherwise relatively low.

In order to make the above vision a reality, it was necessary for Better Place to find a contained setting in which a significant number of electric vehicles could be sold within a limited amount of time. Israel is an ideal test location because of its comparatively small size; all major urban centers are separated by less than 150 km and the majority of its citizens do not travel further than 70 km per day. Supporting Better Place to install the infrastructure necessary for the widespread use of the electric vehicles is also in the strategic interests of Israel as this reduces its reliance on imported oil (Johnson and Suskewicz 2009). The partnership between Better Place, Israel, and Renault-Nissan was announced in January 2008, making Israel the first country to commit to an electric vehicle infrastructure. Ever since then a pilot network deployment began in cooperation with several of Israel's municipalities and in December 2008 Better Place unveiled its first charging spots. Later on Better Place reached agreements with a shopping center group and Israel Railways to place electric vehicle charge spots. In addition, more than 50 companies have signed up to the Better Place scheme in a pledge to replace their current cars with electric vehicles. Given that in Israel 60 percent of new cars are purchased by companies for their employees this should substantially aid the country's transition away from the combustion engine (Johnson and Suskewicz 2009). Specialized GPS software will track battery life and navigate drivers to the nearest charge point or switch station.

Based on the experiences in Israel, Better Place plans to install a similar electric vehicle infrastructure in other countries. The Better Place business model has as a key component a strong service orientation. The company addresses the main issues, which have thus far prevented the more widespread adoption of electric vehicles by offering solutions that fulfill the special service requirements of its customers. In doing so, Better Place hopes to provide the infrastructure necessary to make electric vehicles a convenient and practical alternative means of transportation. Perhaps the biggest issue with the Better Place concept though is the fact that there is no guarantee that the energy used will come from carbon-free sources. If this electricity does not come from a renewable resource, then it is debatable how much has been achieved. What is needed then is a whole system change, in which renewable energy becomes the prominent energy source. The Better Place concept itself, meanwhile, demonstrates the potential of the electric vehicle to be a practical alternative to the fossil fuel combustion engine, and is therefore a superb example of how a single firm explores a new low-carbon business opportunity and paves the way to a more sustainable future.

# 12
# Synthesis
## The mitigation–adaptation nexus

Overall, the carbon crisis constitutes a global, complex, and inter-twined phenomenon. To address the crisis requires transition management (Rotmans and Loorbach 2009), a fundamental change in established structures (e.g., infrastructure), cultures (e.g., collective norms and values), and practices (e.g., production routines). In order to facilitate our understanding and strategic management of the issue this book successively explored three core elements. First, we identified key pathways for the understanding of carbon-induced changes in the business environment. We highlighted the two technology challenges ahead: the decoupling of economic growth from the use of energy and the decarbonization of the energy mix. We emphasized that this requires management to focus on long-term investments and profitability by pursuing three complementary strategies: efficiency, consistency, and sufficiency. Second, we identified the key strategic issues and challenges ahead and emphasized that—although widely established—purely economic approaches have their limitations in addressing and understanding the carbon crisis. Instead, we illustrated that incorporating human, organizational, technological, regulatory, infrastructure, and preparedness elements are essential for paving the way to a low-carbon future.

Notably, we emphasized that this can be achieved without any radical technology breakthroughs. Third, we discussed how to implement effective measures to address the issues adequately: for example, by implementing a carbon management framework and starting inter-firm collaborations. We emphasized that we should learn from the financial crisis and use the knowledge we have in order to prevent a global carbon crisis.

The solutions discussed above address a selection of mitigation options and innovative ideas in order to prevent a global carbon crisis and the severe effects of climate change. Mitigation refers to curbing the human-induced greenhouse gas accumulation in the Earth's atmosphere. However, mitigation policies and efforts at macro, meso, and micro levels will take time to be implemented—especially on a global scale. International consensus needs to be developed on macro policies. Technology change must be accelerated and financing mechanisms have to be fostered for serious mitigation to occur. Firms need to discover the advantage of inter-firm collaborations for carbon reductions and increased competitiveness. And certainly individual managers need to be convinced that proactive strategies to address energy issues and climate change are beneficial. It is also an ongoing academic debate whether the business of business is (only) business and what the role of corporate social responsibility is. This is not what carbon and energy issues are about—they are material. If carbon and energy issues do not affect corporate financial performance to a significant extent yet, they will do so in the near future. They need to be addressed today by adequate risk management. Still we have to acknowledge that all these activities on different levels will take some time to implement. In the meantime climatic changes are already under way, and communities and organizations will be forced to adapt to these changes.

This is not the same kind of adaptation that Darwinians claim as a mechanism of the survival of the fittest. The IPCC (2007b) defines adaptation as adjustment in natural or human systems in response to actual or expected climatic stimuli or their effects, which moderates harm or exploits beneficial opportunities. Humankind can adapt to climate change in three main ways: (1) anticipatory adaptation that takes place before impacts of climate change are observed;

(2) autonomous adaptation that does not constitute a conscious response to climatic stimuli but is triggered by ecological changes in natural systems and by market or welfare changes in human systems; and (3) planned adaptation that is the result of a deliberate policy decision, based on an awareness that conditions have changed or are about to change and that action is required to return to, maintain, or achieve a desired state. These three ways can be illustrated by the ski resorts, which need to adapt to smaller amounts of snow as an effect of global warming and the consequent reduction in the number of commercial skiing days. This is especially the case for ski resorts at lower altitudes. In terms of anticipatory adaptation, a ski resort could build new lifts and slopes at higher altitudes— assuming the option exists geographically. If commercial skiing is not possible at lower altitudes it would still be possible at the facilities located higher up. With respect to autonomous adaptation, more and more ski resorts establish specialized summer programs, which attract tourists during the summer months. Should commercial skiing be impeded, this previously additional source of income may shift towards the main focus of tourism. Regarding planned adaptation, many ski resorts actually pursue a clear adaptation strategy by installing snow machines. The lack of natural snow is compensated for by "industrialized" snow.

The three examples illustrate that adaptation measures can cause further interference with the natural environment, go along with additional business activities, or are even accompanied by significant energy consumption. As such, one central question is how to deal with adaptation that further harms the environment and contributes to climate change. On the one hand, it is important to differentiate between different degrees of necessity for adaptation. In many cases, adaptation is required to protect human beings' health and central systems of modern life. Careful analysis and judgment of necessary and optimal adaptation measures is needed. Furthermore, it is essential to build internal capacity for planned adaptation, which requires companies to change product service offerings, operations, leadership, culture, structure, and systems, as well as rewards and incentives. On the other hand, on all three elaborated levels (macro, meso, micro) there are many cases where adaptation strategies and efforts are implicit in our own solutions. This means that by following a mitigation approach, options for adaptation can be simultaneously incorporated without compromising the prime objective of reducing emissions. For example, by establishing an industrial symbiosis, companies are usually located close to each other. This reduces transportation distances for the required intermediate products and inputs and, thus, adaptation to (i.e., prevention of) potential supply chain disruptions. Similarly, individual companies can build on experienced carbon management teams in order to implement their own adaptation strategy as well as in case of an emergency. Just like in the Hurricane Katrina disaster, Walmart and Home Depot contributed to victims' aid. This illustrates how companies can take the initiative and help mitigate damages in case of an emergency. This may be accompanied by additional costs in the short run; in the long run, however, it contributes to a good corporate reputation. Furthermore, companies can also combine resources across firms to form crisis management teams that respond to large autonomous adaptive events. This bears the potential for cost reductions via mutual learning and collaborative climate risk projects.

Another important question is whether mitigation can take place without adaptation. On the one hand, for example, throughout the book we discussed that climate change will affect African nations the most because of their limited financial resources and their above-average exposure to climatic changes. On the other hand, using Africa in order to install huge arrays of solar panels has been discussed as an important and promising mitigation response. However, will the local inhabitants support Western countries' efforts in curbing greenhouse gas emissions while no one helps them to live with the negative consequences of climate change? Sure, it could be argued that without the efforts of the Western countries the future situation may be even worse. But without balanced adaptation efforts the locals' enthusiasm for such projects will be dampened. This is an important but often missing link when business managers are discussing the feasibility and profitability of only mitigation-focused projects in developing countries. Our suggestion of a global carbon equal fund explicitly incorporates the idea of funding adaptation projects.

We conclude that both mitigation and adaptation are important and inevitable. There is an inherent mitigation–adaptation nexus: adaptation is required as the system is changing; mitigation is required in order to prevent further dangerous changes of the system. The overall strategic objective has to be accelerated mitigation. A completely decarbonized economy may take a long time to establish. That would mean designing human systems with carbon in mind. Everything from buildings, transportation, food, and consumer products would need to be carbon-optimized. Carbon ratings on products may also help consumers choose among products. There is hope that accelerating institutional (i.e., policy, financial markets) and individual (i.e., firms and customers) efforts will establish a decarbonized economy and, as such, large-scale efforts for climate change adaptation become less relevant. However, with the climate system changing rapidly, these accelerated efforts must be made today rather than tomorrow. This requires that every individual and firm acknowledges its role in the carbon crisis and potential to contribute to curbing greenhouse gas emissions. Essentially, there are three simple principles that have to be "lived" within organizations and integrated into the daily decisions of every individual in order to prevent a collapse of the natural environment and the emergence of a global carbon crisis:

- **We do not have to wait further**. Technologies to reduce our carbon footprint exist; decoupling economic growth and energy demand as well as decarbonizing the energy mix are both feasible. We, therefore, do not need to wait for further technologies to be developed and, instead, should accelerate technological application and its diffusion—in developed and in developing countries

- **Realize the low-hanging fruits.** In the business world, there are plenty of examples of actions that increase carbon efficiency and have negative abatement costs, but the required investments are not realized. This phenomenon is referred to as the efficiency paradox (Marechal and Lazaric 2010). In order to address this paradox, the use of "simple" and appropriate technologies is important, which in most cases do not require major new investments—or at least the investments have rather short payback periods

- **Individual action (personal praxis) is important**. This applies within firms as well as for communities. Numerous approaches to measure and reduce personal carbon footprints are available. We just have to realize that each carbon reduction is a contribution to the overall objective: decarbonizing society. A policy instrument such as the suggested global carbon-equal fund may serve as the required incentive for this and at the same time help those financially who need to adapt to climate change now

# References

Alcoforado, M.J., M.D. Nunes, J.C. Garcia, and J.P. Taborda (2000) "Temperature and Precipitation Reconstruction in Southern Portugal During the Late Maunder Minimum (AD 1675–1715)," *Holocene* 10.3: 333-40.

AMAP (2009) *Update on Selected Climate Issues of Concern* (Oslo: Arctic Monitoring and Assessment Programme).

Anderson, B., and C.D. Maria (2010) "Abatement and Allocation in the Pilot Phase of the EU ETS," *Environmental & Resource Economics* 45.1: 83-103.

Angelsen, A., S. Brown, C. Loisel, L. Peskett, C. Streck, and D. Zarin (2009) *Reducing Emissions from Deforestation and Forest Degradation (REDD): An Options Assessment Report* (Washington, DC: Meridian Institute).

Antonelli, C. (1997) "The Economies of Path-Dependence in Industrial Organization," *International Journal of Industrial Organization* 15: 643-75.

ASPO (Association for the Study of Peak Oil and Gas) (2009) *Newsletter No. 100: April 2009* (Uppsala, Sweden: ASPO).

Ayres, R.U., and L.W. Ayres (2002) *A Handbook of Industrial Ecology* (Cheltenham, UK: Edward Elgar).

Bagnall, D.M., and M. Boreland (2008) "Photovoltaic Technologies," *Energy Policy* 36.12: 4,390-96.

Bala, G., K. Caldeira, M. Wickett, T.J. Phillips, D.B. Lobell, C. Delire, and A. Mirin (2007) "Combined Climate and Carbon-cycle Effects of Large-scale Deforestation," *Proceedings of the National Academy of Sciences* 140.16: 6,550-55.

Bansal, P., and K. Roth (2000) "Why Companies Go Green: A Model of Ecological Responsiveness," *Academy of Management Journal* 43.4: 717-36.

Baron, R. (2006) *Sectoral Approaches to GHG Mitigation: Scenarios for Integration* (Paris: OECD/IEA).

Baumol, W.J. (1972) "On Taxation and the Control of Externalities," *American Economic Review* 62.3: 307-22.

Bloomfield, S. (2006) "Africa 'will be worst hit by climate change'," *The Independent*, 6 November 2006.

Boulding, K.E. (1966) "The Economics of the Coming Spaceship Earth," in H. Jarrett (ed.), *Environmental Quality in a Growing Economy* (Baltimore, MD: Johns Hopkins University Press): 3-14.

Broecker, W.S. (2001) "Was the Medieval Warm Period Global?" *Science* 291.5508: 1,497-99.

Bullis, K. (2008) *Making Electric Vehicles Practical: New Infrastructure May Help Launch Electric Cars in Israel and Denmark* (Cambridge, MA: MIT Technology Review).

Busch, T. (2010) "Carbon Performance Indicators Revisited," *Journal of Industrial Ecology* 14.3: 374-77.

—— and V.H. Hoffmann (2007) "Emerging Carbon Constraints for Corporate Risk Management," *Ecological Economics* 62.3-4: 518-28.

——, H. Klee, and V.H. Hoffmann (2008) "Curbing Greenhouse Gas Emissions on a Sectoral Basis: The Cement Sustainability Initiative," in R. Sullivan (ed.), *Corporate Responses to Climate Change* (Sheffield, UK: Greenleaf Publishing): 204-19.

Carter, B. (2006) "There IS a problem with global warming . . . it stopped in 1998," Personal View, www.telegraph.co.uk/comment/personal-view/3624242/There-IS-a-problem-with-global-warming...-it-stopped-in-1998.html#, accessed February 15, 2011.

CDP (Carbon Disclosure Project) (2010) *Carbon Disclosure Project 2010: Global 500 Report* (London: CDP).

Chamberlain, G. (2009) "India Prays for Rain as Water Wars Break Out," www.guardian.co.uk/world/2009/jul/12/india-water-supply-bhopal, accessed March 25, 2011.

Chatterjee, R. (2009) "The Road to REDD," *Environmental Science & Technology* 43: 557-60.

Chen, S., and M. Ravallion (2008) *The Developing World is Poorer Than We Thought, But No Less Successful in the Fight Against Poverty* (Washington, DC: The World Bank Development Research Group).

Cohen, M.A., and M.P. Vandenbergh (2008) *Consumption, Happiness, and Climate Change* (Washington, DC: Resources for the Future Discussion Paper).

Crowley, T.J., and T.S. Lowery (2000) "How Warm Was the Medieval Warm Period?" *Ambio* 29.1: 51-54.

Daly, H.E. (1973) *Toward a Steady-state Economy* (San Francisco: Freeman).

Deffeyes, K.S. (2005) *Beyond Oil: The View from Hubbert's Peak* (New York: Farrar, Straus & Giroux).

Dell, M., B.F. Jones, and B.A. Olken (2008) *Climate Change and Economic Growth: Evidence from the Last Half Century* (Cambridge, MA: National Bureau of Economic Research).

DESERTEC Foundation (2009) *Clean Power from Deserts: The DESERTEC Concept for Energy, Water and Climate Security* (Hamburg, Germany: DESERTEC Foundation).

DiMaggio, P.J., and W.W. Powell (1983) "The Iron Cage Revisited: Institutional Isomorphism and Collective Rationality in Organizational Fields," *American Sociological Review* 48.2: 147-60.

Doh, J.P., S.D. Howton, S.W. Howton, and D.S. Siegel (2010) "Does the Market Respond to an Endorsement of Social Responsibility? The Role of Institutions, Information, and Legitimacy," *Journal of Management* 36.6: 1,461-85.

ECF (2010) *Roadmap 2050: A Practical Guide to a Prosperous Low-carbon Europe* (Den Haag: European Climate Foundation).

*Economist, The* (2008) "Plumbing the Depths: OPEC has its work cut out to stop the oil price from sinking further," *The Economist* 4 December 2008.

Ehrlich, P.R., and J.P. Holdren (1971) "Impact of Population Growth," *Science* 171.3977: 1,212-17.

Ellerman, A.D., and B.K. Buchner (2008) "Over-allocation or Abatement? A Preliminary Analysis of the EU ETS Based on the 2005–06 Emissions Data," *Environmental & Resource Economics* 41.2: 267-87.

—— and P.L. Joskow (2008) *The European Union's Emissions Trading System in Perspective* (Arlington, VA: Pew Center on Global Climate Change).

Engau, C., and V.H. Hoffmann (2009) "Effects of Regulatory Uncertainty on Corporate Strategy: An Analysis of Firm Responses to Uncertainty about Post-Kyoto Policy," *Environmental Science & Policy* 12: 766-77.

EPIA (European Photovoltaic Industry Association) (2009) *Global Market Outlook for Photovoltaics until 2013* (Brussels: EPIA).

Felder, S., and T.F. Rutherford (1993) "Unilateral $CO_2$ Reductions and Carbon Leakage: The Consequences of International-Trade in Oil and Basic Materials," *Journal of Environmental Economics and Management* 25.2: 162-76.

George, S. (2010) *Whose Crisis, Whose Future?* (Cambridge, UK: Polity Press).

German Aerospace Center (2005) *Concentrating Solar Power for the Mediterranean Region* (Stuttgart: German Aerospace Center).

Global Footprint Network (2011) "National Footprint Accounts," 2010 edition, www.footprintnetwork.org, accessed March 3, 2011.

Graedel, T.E., and B.R. Allenby (2003) *Industrial Ecology* (Upper Saddle River, NJ: Prentice-Hall, 2nd edn).

Gulledge, J. (2008) "Climate Change Risks in the Context of Scientific Uncertainty," in K.M. Campbell and J. Price (eds.), *The Global Politics of Energy* (Washington, DC: The Aspen Institute): 115-32.

Harmeling, S., and B. Müller (2011) "What to do now?" Oxford Energy and Environment Brief, The Oxford Institute for Energy Studies, www.oxfordenergy.org/pdfs/comment_02_01_11.pdf, accessed March 25, 2011.

Hart, S.L. (1995) "A Natural-Resource-Based View of the Firm," *Academy of Management Review* 20.4: 986-1,014.

Hashimoto, S. (2004) *Analysis of Strategies of Companies under Carbon Constraint: Relationship between Profit Structure of Companies and Carbon/ Fuel Price Uncertainty* (Cambridge, MA: MIT Joint Program on the Science and Policy of Global Change).

Haughton, J., and S.R. Khandker (2009) *Handbook on Poverty and Inequality* (Washington, DC: World Bank).

Hegerl, G.C., and S. Solomon (2009) "Risks of Climate Engineering," *Science* 325: 955-56.

Hirsch, R., R. Bezdek, and R. Wendling (2005) *Peaking of World Oil Production: Impacts, Mitigation, and Risk Management* (Pittsburgh, PA: DOE NETL).

Hoffman, A.J. (1999) "Institutional Evolution and Change: Environmentalism and the US Chemical Industry," *Academy of Management Journal* 42.4: 351-71.

—— (2005) "Climate Change Strategy: The Business Logic Behind Voluntary Greenhouse Gas Reductions," *California Management Review* 47.3: 21-46.

—— (2006) *Getting Ahead of the Curve: Corporate Strategies that Address Climate Change* (Arlington, VA: Pew Center on Global Climate Change).

Hoffmann, V.H., and T. Busch (2007) "Carbon Constraints in the 14th and 21st Century," *Journal of Industrial Ecology* 11.2: 4-6.

—— and T. Busch (2008) "Corporate Carbon Performance Indicators: Carbon Intensity, Dependency, Exposure, and Risk," *Journal of Industrial Ecology* 12.4: 505-20.

——, T. Trautmann, and J. Hamprecht (2009) "Regulatory Uncertainty: A Reason to Postpone Investments? Not Necessarily," *Journal of Management Studies* 46.7: 1,227-53.

Hotelling, H. (1931) "The Economics of Exhaustible Resources," *Journal of Political Economy* 39: 137-75.

Hubbert, M.K. (1956) *Nuclear Energy and the Fossil Fuels* (Houston, TX: Shell Development Company).

Huber, J. (2000) "Industrielle Ökologie: Konsistenz, Effizienz und Suffizienz in zyklusanalytischer Betrachtung," in R. Kreibich and U.E. Simonis (eds.), *Global Change* (Berlin: Berlin Verlag Arno Spitz): 109-26.

IEA (International Energy Agency) (2006) *World Energy Outlook 2006* (Paris: IEA).

—— (2008) *World Energy Outlook 2008* (Paris: IEA).

IMF (2009) "World Economic Outlook Update: Global Economic Slump Challenges Policies," www.imf.org/external/pubs/ft/weo/2009/update/01/index.htm, accessed March 24, 2011.

IPCC (Intergovernmental Panel on Climate Change) (2001) *Climate Change 2001—Working Group I: The Scientific Basis* (Cambridge, UK: Cambridge University Press).

—— (2005) *Carbon Dioxide Capture and Storage* (Cambridge, UK: Cambridge University Press).

—— (2007a) *Climate Change 2007: Impacts, Adaptation and Vulnerability* (Geneva: IPCC).

—— (2007b) *Climate Change 2007: Synthesis Report* (Geneva: IPCC).

—— (2007c) *Climate Change 2007: The Physical Science Basis* (Cambridge, UK: Cambridge University Press).

ITPOES (UK Industry Taskforce on Peak Oil & Energy Security) (2010) *The Oil Crunch: A Wake-up Call for the UK Economy* (London: UK ITPOES).

Jacobsen, N.B. (2006) "Industrial Symbiosis in Kalundborg, Denmark: A Quantitative Assessment of Economic and Environmental Aspects," *Journal of Industrial Ecology* 10.1-2: 239-55.

Jeswani, H.K., W. Wehrmeyer, and Y. Mulugetta (2008) "How Warm is the Corporate Response to Climate Change? Evidence from Pakistan and the UK," *Business Strategy and the Environment* 17.1: 46-60.

Johnson, M.W., and J. Suskewicz (2009) "How to Jump-Start the Clean-Tech Economy," *Harvard Business Review* 87.11: 52-60.

Johnston, T.C., and J.B. Burton (2003) "Voluntary Simplicity: Definitions and Dimensions," *Academy of Marketing Studies Journal* 7.1: 19-36.

Keigwin, L.D. (1996) "The Little Ice Age and Medieval Warm Period in the Sargasso Sea," *Science* 274.5292: 1,504-508.

—— and R.S. Pickart (1999) "Slope Water Current over the Laurentian Fan on Interannual to Millennial Time Scales," *Science* 286.5439: 520-23.

Knigge, M., and B. Görlach (2005) *Effects of Germany's Ecological Tax Reforms on the Environment, Employment and Technological Innovation* (Berlin: Institute for International and European Environmental Policy, www.umweltbundesamt.de/uba-info-presse-e/hintergrund/oekosteuer.pdf).

Kolk, A., and V.H. Hoffmann (2007) "Business, Climate Change and Emissions Trading: Taking Stock and Looking Ahead," *European Management Journal* 25.6: 411-14.

—— and J. Pinkse (2005) "Business Responses to Climate Change: Identifying Emergent Strategies," *California Management Review* 47.3: 6-20.

—— and J. Pinkse (2007) "Towards Strategic Stakeholder Management? Integrating Perspectives on Sustainability Challenges such as Corporate Responses to Climate Change," *Corporate Governance* 7.4: 370-78.

Lashof, D.A. (1989) "The Dynamic Greenhouse: Feedback Processes that May Influence Future Concentrations of Atmospheric Trace Gases and Climatic Change," *Climatic Change* 14.3: 213-42.

Levy, D.L. (2010) "It's The Real Thing: The Power of Koch," climateinc. org/2010/09/koch_climate/, accessed September 8, 2010.

Lovins, A.B., E.K. Datta, O.-E. Bustnes, J.G. Koomey, and N.J. Glasgow (2005) *Winning the Oil Endgame* (Snowmass, CO: Rocky Mountain Institute).

Lowe, R. (2000) "Defining and Meeting the Carbon Constraints of the 21st Century," *Building Research & Information* 28.3: 159-75.

Mabey, N., and J. Mitchell (2010) *Investing for an Uncertain Future: Priorities for UK Energy and Climate Security* (London: Chatham House).

McGuigan, C., R. Reynolds and D. Wiedmer (2002) "Poverty and Climate Change: Assessing Impacts in Developing Countries and the Initiatives of the International Community," Consultancy Project for the Overseas Development Institute, London School of Economics, www.odi.org.uk/iedg/publications/inter_negs_wps.html, accessed March 25, 2011.

McKinsey (2009) *Pathways to a Low-Carbon Economy: Version 2 of the Global Greenhouse Gas Abatement Cost Curve* (New York: McKinsey & Company).

Mangan, A., and E. Olivetti (2008) *By-product Synergy Networks, Driving Innovation through Waste Reduction and Carbon Mitigation* (Austin, TX: US Business Council for Sustainable Development; Cambridge, MA: Massachusetts Institute of Technology).

Mann, M.E. (2002) "Little Ice Age," in M.C. MacCracken and J.S. Perry (eds.), *Encyclopedia of Global Environmental Change* (Chichester, UK: John Wiley): 504-509.

Marechal, K., and N. Lazaric (2010) "Overcoming Inertia: Insights from Evolutionary Economics into Improved Energy and Climate Policies," *Climate Policy* 10: 103-19.

Matthews, H.D., and A.J. Weaver (2010) "Committed Climate Warming," *Nature Geoscience* 3: 142-43.

Meadows, D.H., D.L. Meadows, J. Randers and W.W. Behrens (1972) *The Limits to Growth* (New York: Universe Books).

Meyer, J.W., and B. Rowan (1977) "Institutionalized Organizations: Formal-Structure as Myth and Ceremony," *American Journal of Sociology* 83.2: 340-63.

Morris, D., and B. Worthington (2010) *Cap or Trap? How the EU ETS Risks Locking-in Carbon Emissions* (London: Sandbag).

Nader, S. (2009) "Paths to a Low-carbon Economy: The Masdar Example," *Energy Procedia* 1: 3,951-58.

Nelson, R.R. (1991) "Why Do Firms Differ, and How Does It Matter?" *Strategic Management Journal* 12: 61-74.

Okereke, C. (2007) "An Exploration of Motivations, Drivers and Barriers to Carbon Management: The UK FTSE 100," *European Management Journal* 25.6: 475-86.

Oliver, C. (1991) "Strategic Responses to Institutional Processes," *Academy of Management Review* 16.1: 145-79.

Orsato, R. (2006) "Competitive Environmental Strategies: When Does It Pay to be Green?" *California Management Review* 48.2: 127-43.

Pfeffer, W.T., J.T. Harper, and S. O'Neel (2008) "Kinematic Constraints on Glacier Contributions to 21st-Century Sea-level Rise," *Science* 321.5894: 1,340-43.

Porter, M.E. (1980) *Competitive Strategy: Techniques for Analyzing Industries and Competitors* (New York: Free Press).

—— and F.L. Reinhardt (2007) "A Strategic Approach to Climate," *Harvard Business Review* 85.10: 22-26.

Powell, W.W., and P.J. DiMaggio (1991) *The New Institutionalism in Organizational Analysis* (Chicago: University of Chicago Press).

Prins, G., I. Galiana, C. Green, R. Grundman, M. Hulme, A. Korhola F. Laird, T. Nordhaus, R. Pielke Jr, S. Rayner, D. Sarewitz, M. Shellenberger, N. Stehr, and H. Tezuka (2010) *The Hartwell Paper: A New Direction for Climate Policy after the Crash of 2009* (Oxford, UK: University of Oxford; London: London School of Economics).

Quaschning, V. (2010) *Renewable Energy and Climate Change* (Chichester, UK: John Wiley).

Rahmstorf, S. (2007) "A Semi-empirical Approach to Projecting Future Sea-level Rise," *Science* 315.5810: 368-70.

Raupach, M.R., G. Marland, P. Ciais, C. Le Quéré, J.G. Canadell, G. Klepper, and C.B. Field (2007) "Global and Regional Drivers of Accelerating $CO_2$ Emissions," *Proceedings of the National Academy of Sciences* 104.24: 10,288-93.

Rayner, S. (2010) "How to Eat an Elephant: A Bottom-up Approach to Climate Policy," *Climate Policy* 10: 615-21.

Reiche, D. (2009) "Renewable Energy Policies in the Gulf Countries: A Case Study of the Carbon-Neutral 'Masdar City' in Abu Dhabi," *Energy Policy* 38.1: 378-82.

Reynolds, A. (2002) *Warnings from the Bush: The Impact of Climate Change on the Nature of Australia* (Ultimo, NSW: Climate Action Network Australia).

Reynolds, D. (1999) "The Mineral Economy: How Prices and Costs can Falsely Signal Decreasing Scarcity," *Ecological Economics* 31.1: 155-66.

Roberts, J.A. (1996) "Green Consumers in the 1990s: Profile and Implications for Advertising," *Journal of Business Research* 36.3: 217-31.

Rosen, S. (1974) "Hedonic Prices and Implicit Markets: Product Differentiation in Pure Competition," *Journal of Political Economy* 82.1: 34-55.

Rotmans, J., and D. Loorbach (2009) "Complexity and Transition Management," *Journal of Industrial Ecology* 13.2: 184-96.

Royal Society, The (2009) *Geoengineering the Climate: Science, Governance and Uncertainty* (London: The Royal Society).

Russo, M.V., and P.A. Fouts (1997) "A Resource-based Perspective on Corporate Environmental Performance and Profitability," *Academy of Management Journal* 40.3: 534-59.

Ruth, M. (2006) "A Quest for the Economics of Sustainability and the Sustainability of Economics," *Ecological Economics* 56: 332-42.

Schultz, K., and P. Williamson (2005) "Gaining Competitive Advantage in a Carbon-Constrained World: Strategies for European Business," *European Management Journal* 23.4: 383-91.

Schwierz, C., P. Köllner-Heck, E.Z. Mutter, D.N. Bresch, P.-L. Vidale, M. Wild, and C. Schär (2009) "Modelling European Winter Wind Storm Losses in Current and Future Climate," *Climatic Change* 101.3–4: 485-514.

Scnat (Forum of the Swiss Academy of Sciences) (2010) "The Arguments of the Climate Skeptics," Climate Press No. 29, proclim4f.scnat.ch/4dcgi/proclim/de/News?1501 (in German), accessed March 25, 2011.

Scott, A., and P. Pearse (1992) "Natural Resources in a High-tech Economy: Scarcity versus Resourcefulness," *Resources Policy* 18.3: 154-66.

Scott, W.R. (2001) *Institutions and Organizations* (London: Sage Publications, 2nd edn).

Shrivastava, P. (1992) *Bhopal: Anatomy of a Crisis* (Vol. 2; London: Paul Chapman Publishing).

—— (1995a) "Ecocentric Management for a Risk Society," *Academy of Management Review* 20.1: 118-37.

—— (1995b) "Environmental Technologies and Competitive Advantage," *Strategic Management Journal* 16: 183-200.

—— (1995c) "The Role of Corporations in Achieving Ecological Sustainability," *Academy of Management Review* 20.4: 936-60.

——, I.I. Mitroff, D. Miller and A. Miglani (1988) "Understanding Industrial Crisis," *Journal of Management Studies* 25.4: 285-304.

Sills, J. (2010) "Climate Change and the Integrity of Science," *Science* 328.5979: 689-90.

Socolow, R., R. Hotinski, J.B. Greenblatt, and S. Pacala (2004) "Solving the Climate Problem: Technologies Available to Curb $CO_2$ Emissions," *Environment* 46.10: 8-19.

Solomon, S., G.-K. Plattner, R. Knutti, and P. Friedlingstein (2009) "Irreversible Climate Change due to Carbon Dioxide Emissions," *Proceedings of the National Academy of Sciences* 106.6: 1,704-709.

Sorrell, S., J. Speirs, R. Bentley, A. Brandt, and R. Miller (2009) *An Assessment of the Evidence for a Near-term Peak in Global Oil Production* (London: UK Energy Research Centre).

——, J. Speirs, R. Bentley, A. Brandt, and R. Miller (2010) "Global Oil Depletion: A Review of the Evidence," *Energy Policy* 38.9: 5,290-95.

Stern, N. (2006) *The Economics of Climate Change: The Stern Review* (Cambridge, UK: Cambridge University Press).

Stoft, S. (2008) *Carbonomics: How to Fix the Climate and Charge It to OPEC* (Nantucket, MA: Diamond Press).

Sturcken, E. (2010) "Walmart Releases Its Roadmap to GHG Accounting," ClimateBiz, www.greenbiz.com/blog/2010/08/05/walmart-releases-its-roadmap-ghg-accounting?page=full, accessed August 5, 2010.

Suchman, M.C. (1995) "Managing Legitimacy: Strategic and Institutional Approaches," *Academy of Management Review* 20.3: 571-610.

Swiss Re (2006) *The Effects of Climate Change: Storm Damage in Europe on the Rise* (Zurich: Swiss Reinsurance Company).

TEEB (The Economics of Ecosystems and Biodiversity) (2010) *The Economics of Ecosystems and Biodiversity: Report for Business* (Bonn: TEEB, UNEP).

Tierney, J. (1990) "Betting the Planet," *New York Times Magazine*, December 2, 1990: 52 (Section 6).

Tol, R.S.J. (2003) "Is the Uncertainty about Climate Change too Large for Expected Cost–Benefit Analysis?" *Climatic Change* 56.3: 265-89.

—— (2008) "The Social Cost of Carbon: Trends, Outliers and Catastrophes," *Economics* 2.25: 1-22.

Trudel, R., and J. Cotte (2009) "Does It Pay To Be Good?" *MIT Sloan Management Review* 50.2: 61-68.

UN (United Nations) (2007) *The Millennium Development Goals Report* (New York: United Nations).

—— (2010) *World Economic Situation and Prospects 2010* (New York: United Nations).

UNDP (United Nations Development Programme) (2007) *Human Development Report 2007/2008* (New York: UNDP).

Unruh, G.C. (2000) "Understanding Carbon Lock-in," *Energy Policy* 28.12: 817-30.

Valdez, S. (2000) *An Introduction to Global Financial Markets* (New York: Palgrave, 3rd edn).

—— (2007) *An Introduction to Global Financial Markets* (New York: Palgrave Macmillan, 5th edn).

Vidal, J. (2009) "Redd in Africa: 'How we can earn money from air by harvesting carbon?'" www.guardian.co.uk/environment/2009/oct/05/redd-kenya-climate-change, accessed March 25, 2011.

WBCSD (World Business Council for Sustainable Development) (2009) *Transforming the Market: Energy Efficiency in Buildings* (Geneva: WBCSD).

—— and WRI (2004) *The Greenhouse Gas Protocol: A Corporate Accounting and Reporting Standard* (Geneva: WBCSD; Washington, DC: World Resources Institute, revised version).

Weiss, E.B. (1989) *In Fairness to Future Generations: International Law, Common Patrimony and Intergenerational Equity* (Tokyo: The United Nations University).

Wigley, T.M.L. (2005) "The Climate Change Commitment," *Science* 307: 1,766-69.

World Bank (2009) *World Development Report* (Washington, DC: World Bank).

Zeller, T. (2009) "Europe Looks to Africa for Solar Power," *The New York Times*, June 22, 2009.

Zhang, Y.J., and Y.M. Wei (2010) "An Overview of Current Research on the EU ETS: Evidence from its Operating Mechanism and Economic Effect," *Applied Energy* 87: 1,804-14.

Zimmer, M.R., T.F. Stafford, and M.R. Stafford (1994) "Green Issues: Dimensions of Environmental Concern," *Journal of Business Research* 30.1: 63-74.

# Glossary

| | |
|---|---|
| Abatement cost (McKinsey 2009) | The carbon abatement cost curve reflects the annualized cost of different abatement measures in a given year per tonne of carbon saved compared with the business-as-usual technology. This metric allows comparing the economic attractiveness of different abatement measures |
| Adaptation (www.ipcc.ch/pdf/glossary/tar-ipcc-terms-en.pdf) | Adjustment in natural or human systems to a new or changing environment. Adaptation to climate change refers to adjustment in natural or human systems in response to actual or expected climatic stimuli or their effects, which moderates harm or exploits beneficial opportunities. Various types of adaptation can be distinguished, including anticipatory and reactive adaptation, private and public adaptation, and autonomous and planned adaptation |
| Afforestation (www.ipcc.ch/pdf/glossary/tar-ipcc-terms-en.pdf) | Planting of new forests on lands that historically have not contained forests |

| Carbon constraints (Busch and Hoffmann 2007) | Carbon constraints are any limitations companies face regarding established utilization patterns of the element carbon that impact business conditions. These limitations pertain to direct, physical effects (e.g., supply chain disruptions due to weather extremes) as well as to indirect, human-induced effects (e.g., climate change legislation) |
| --- | --- |
| Carbon efficiency (Hoffmann and Busch 2008) | Companies use fossil fuels and emit greenhouse gases. As such, they use carbon-based inputs and emit carbon-containing outputs. By increasing their carbon efficiency they are able to optimize both carbon in- and outputs. As carbon inputs have a market price and carbon outputs are increasingly subject to regulation such as taxes, an efficient use of carbon matters financially for companies in two ways. A firm can compare the carbon efficiency, for example, of two production processes by considering how much carbon was required for generating the output of each process (e.g., a specific component). However, for the carbon performance assessments of companies, four carbon performance indicators are more useful: carbon intensity, dependency, exposure, and risk |
| Carbon dependency (Hoffmann and Busch 2008) | This ratio is based on a firm's carbon intensity for two different years. By considering both intensities, the firm's carbon dependency allows assessment of the extent to which a firm's physical carbon performance has changed over time. This indicator is of special interest for policy makers: based on such information they are able to evaluate the effectiveness of climate policies in terms of the achieved carbon reductions by individual firms or in specific sectors |

| | |
|---|---|
| Carbon exposure (Hoffmann and Busch 2008) | This ratio is based on a firm's carbon intensity for a given year. It relates a company's carbon costs to another financial metric (e.g., sales). The carbon costs comprise the costs for fossil fuels (carbon inputs) as well as potential costs relating to the emission of GHGs (carbon outputs), for example, in the case of the European Union Emissions Trading Scheme. The ratio allows comparisons between companies regarding the financial implications of their carbon use for a given time period |
| Carbon intensity (Hoffmann and Busch 2008) | This ratio relates a firm's carbon usage, usually measured in terms of its greenhouse gas emissions, to its business performance. It is calculated as the firm's carbon usage for a given year divided by a financial metric (e.g., sales) for the same time period. The ratio allows comparisons between companies regarding their relative physical carbon performance at a given time |
| Carbon leakage (www.ipcc.ch/pdf/ glossary/tar-ipcc-terms-en.pdf) | The part of emissions reductions in one country that may be offset by an increase in the emissions in another country. This can occur through: (1) relocation of energy-intensive production in non-constrained regions; (2) increased consumption of fossil fuels in these regions through decline in the international price of oil and gas triggered by lower demand for these fuels; and (3) changes in incomes (thus in energy demand) because of better terms of trade. Leakage also refers to the situation in which a carbon sequestration activity (e.g., tree planting) on one piece of land inadvertently, directly or indirectly, triggers an activity, which in whole or part, counteracts the carbon effects of the initial activity |

| | |
|---|---|
| Carbon risk (Hoffmann and Busch 2008) | This ratio is based on a firm's carbon exposure for two different years. By considering both exposure values, the firm's carbon risk allows assessment of the extent to which the financial implications of a firm's carbon usage have changed over time. This indicator is of special interest for financial analysts: based on such information they are able to evaluate the carbon risks of different portfolios and investments and which companies are managing their climate liabilities appropriately |
| Climate feedback (www.ipcc.ch/pdf/ glossary/tar-ipcc-terms-en.pdf) | An interaction mechanism between processes in the climate system is called a climate feedback, when the result of an initial process triggers changes in a second process that in turn influences the initial one. A feedback can either intensify the original process, or reduce it |
| Deforestation (www.ipcc.ch/pdf/ glossary/tar-ipcc-terms-en.pdf) | Conversion of forest to non-forest |
| GHG (www.ipcc.ch/pdf/ glossary/tar-ipcc-terms-en.pdf) | Greenhouse gases are those gaseous constituents of the atmosphere, both natural and anthropogenic, that absorb and emit radiation at specific wavelengths within the spectrum of infrared radiation emitted by the Earth's surface, the atmosphere, and clouds. This property causes the greenhouse effect. Water vapor ($H_2O$), carbon dioxide ($CO_2$), nitrous oxide ($N_2O$), methane ($CH_4$), and ozone ($O_3$) are the primary greenhouse gases in the Earth's atmosphere. Moreover there are a number of entirely human-made greenhouse gases in the atmosphere, such as the halocarbons and other chlorine- and bromine-containing substances, dealt with under the Montreal Protocol. Besides $CO_2$, $N_2O$, and $CH_4$, the Kyoto Protocol deals with the greenhouse gases sulfur hexafluoride ($SF_6$), hydrofluorocarbons (HFCs), and perfluorocarbons (PFCs) |

| | |
|---|---|
| Kyoto Protocol (www.ipcc.ch/pdf/ glossary/tar-ipcc-terms-en.pdf) | The Kyoto Protocol to the United Nations Framework Convention on Climate Change was adopted at the Conference of the Parties in 1997 in Kyoto, Japan. It contains legally binding commitments for countries that signed it. Countries included in Annex B of the Protocol (most countries in the Organisation for Economic Co-operation and Development, and countries with economies in transition) agreed to reduce their anthropogenic greenhouse gas emissions by at least 5 percent below 1990 levels in the commitment period 2008 to 2012 |
| Low-carbon innovations | In response to emerging carbon constraints companies should seek to develop low-carbon innovations. Such innovations can be processed-based (e.g., substitution of fossil fuel in a production system) or product-/service-oriented (e.g., end-products that emit only a minimum of carbon dioxide). Low-carbon innovations can generate competitive benefits in an increasingly carbon-constrained business environment |
| Mitigation (www.ipcc.ch/pdf/ glossary/tar-ipcc-terms-en.pdf) | An anthropogenic intervention to reduce the sources or enhance the sinks of greenhouse gases |
| Montreal Protocol (www.ipcc.ch/pdf/ glossary/tar-ipcc-terms-en.pdf) | The Montreal Protocol on substances that deplete the ozone layer was adopted in Montreal in 1987. It controls the consumption and production of chlorine- and bromine-containing chemicals that destroy stratospheric ozone, such as chlorofluorocarbons (CFCs), methyl chloroform, carbon tetrachloride, and many others |

| | |
|---|---|
| Peak oil<br>(Hubbert 1956) | The term peak oil is usually used to refer to the depletion mid-point. This is the point in time after which half of the available resources of a fossil fuel have been used |
| Scope<br>(WBCSD and WRI 2004) | The Greenhouse Gas Protocol Initiative developed three scopes to measure a firm's GHG emissions. Scope 1 takes a "gate-to-gate" view and comprises all direct emissions: e.g., stemming from a firm's internal heating system. Scope 2 accounts for all emissions that are related to the firm's energy purchases: e.g., the GHGs that were emitted by the electricity generation by an independent (i.e., third-party-owned) energy utility. Scope 3 ideally includes all further emissions that can be ascribed to a firm's business activities when taking a full-life-cycle perspective. As such, they would include suppliers' emissions, transportation, etc. In reality it is difficult to precisely determine all Scope 3 emissions |
| Reforestation<br>(www.ipcc.ch/pdf/<br>glossary/tar-ipcc-terms-<br>en.pdf) | Planting of forests on lands that have previously contained forests but that have been converted to some other use |
| Sequestration<br>(www.ipcc.ch/pdf/<br>glossary/tar-ipcc-terms-<br>en.pdf) | The process of increasing the carbon content of a carbon reservoir other than the atmosphere. Biological approaches to sequestration include direct removal of carbon dioxide from the atmosphere through land-use change, afforestation, reforestation, and practices that enhance soil carbon in agriculture. Physical approaches include separation and disposal of carbon dioxide from flue gases or from processing fossil fuels to produce hydrogen- and carbon-dioxide-rich fractions and long-term storage underground in depleted oil and gas reservoirs, coal seams, and saline aquifers |

# Index

Page numbers in *italic figures* refer to figures and tables

# About the authors

**Dr. Timo Busch** is currently working as a lecturer and senior researcher at the Swiss Federal Institute of Technology (ETH) in Zurich, Switzerland. His research interests include corporate strategies towards a low-carbon economy, organizational adaptation to climate change, and the business case for corporate environmental sustainability. He teaches at ETH and Duisenberg School of Finance (The Netherlands) courses on corporate sustainability, strategy, and finance. The topic of his PhD thesis was strategic management under carbon constraints. Before joining ETH Timo worked at the Wuppertal Institute for Climate, Environment and Energy (Germany) focusing on corporate eco-efficiency, life cycle analyses, and sustainable finance. His work has been published in international journals including: the *Journal of Industrial Ecology*; *Ecological Economics*; *Business & Society*; *Business Strategy and the Environment*; and the *Journal of Business Ethics*.

**Dr. Paul Shrivastava** is the David O'Brien Distinguished Professor of Sustainable Enterprise, and Director of the David O'Brien Centre for Sustainable Enterprise at the John Molson School of Business, Concordia University, Montreal, Canada. He is Senior Advisor on sustainability to Bucknell University and the Indian Institute of Management Shillong, India. Paul received his PhD from the University of Pittsburgh. He was tenured Associate Professor of Management at the Stern School of Business, New York University. He has published 15 books and over 100 articles in professional journals. He has served on the editorial boards of leading management education journals including: the *Academy of Management Review*; the *Strategic Management Journal*; *Organization*; *Risk Management*; *Business Strategy and the Environment*; and the *International Journal of Sustainable Strategic Management*. He won a Fulbright Senior Scholar Award. His work has been featured in the *Los Angeles Times*, the *Philadelphia Inquirer*, the *Christian Science Monitor*, and on the McNeil/Lehrer NewsHour.

For Product Safety Concerns and Information please contact our EU
representative GPSR@taylorandfrancis.com Taylor & Francis Verlag GmbH,
Kaufingerstraße 24, 80331 München, Germany

Printed and bound by CPI Group (UK) Ltd, Croydon, CR0 4YY

01/05/2025

01858374-0001